WALK FOR JUSTICE

One's man sacrifice for
another man's freedom

By

Harry "Goodwolf" Kindness

Wo-Pila Publishing
Erie, Pennsylvania

Library of Congress Catalog Card Number: 99-070912

Kindness, Harry "Good Wolf"
        Walk for Justice
                One man's sacrifice for another man's freedom

ISBN: 1-886340-99-4

TABLE OF CONTENTS

Acknowledgments

I would like to thank Manny Twofeathers and his family, for help getting this project off the ground, especially Manny's wife, Melody Rendon for all the time she spent editing and researching this book. Rod Jackson for his input and editing while going down Highway 50 with me.

To Dennis Banks and all the members of the American Indian Movement for giving me the opportunity to complete this endeavor - without them it would not have been possible. Special thanks goes to the numerous participants and supporters of the "Walk for Justice" for all their efforts and assistance.

Tommy Caputo, many thanks for your inspiration, support, contributions and many late nights spent working on this project.

To my family and all their support in everything I do.

And words can hardly express how grateful I am to my dearest wife, Karen for the unselfish and unending support in everything I do. Without her, I wouldn't be here today.

INTRODUCTION

Many people have asked me what made me decide to walk across the United States. This is the best way I can explain. I was reading "News from Indian Country" (a bi-monthly Native American newspaper) and spotted an article put out by the American Indian Movement (A.I.M.) announcing a Spiritual Walk across the United States. It was to bring attention to Leonard Peltier's case and other indigenous matters to be brought before the United States Congress in Washington. There was a telephone number to contact Dennis Bank's office in Kentucky for more information.

Being an old school A.I.M. member and knowing Leonard Peltier personally, I called to find out what I had to do to participate. I had not been involved with A.I.M. since 1972. I was living in Las Vegas, Nevada with my wife, where life was fast and high. One can get caught up in this life very easily. You lose a sense of what is really happening with mainstream life and sometimes lose yourself as a human being and what you're here to do.

One night on my way to a club with my friend, Tommy, I talked it over with him about maybe participating in the walk. He felt it would accomplish two things. It would reacquaint me with my Indian heritage and would help prepare me physically and mentally for the Sundance I would be participating in August.

His reasoning was right, it was time for me to

get back on the Red Road. At the time, I was involved in all kinds of nefarious activities that were the complete opposite of my last name "Kindness". The only good thing happening in my life at this time was my wife, Karen. She has stood by me through some hard times and helped get me back on the right path. This would give me a chance to get back on track, and do something that had a deep meaning that was close to my heart.

Originally I only planned to walk two weeks to one month. I came off this walk a better person spiritually, mentally and physically. I felt like a true Native American. Perhaps when you share this with me, somehow you'll come out of it a better person in knowing what can be accomplished, and how we can all make a difference if we only try.

So come along, and join me on Highway 50 on this 3,800 mile spiritual journey across America, known as the "Walk for Justice."

CALIFORNIA

My name is Harry Kindness. I am a forty-seven year old Native American from the Oneida tribe. At the time of this **Walk for Justice** I was forty-two years old. This is the true story of the Walk that began on February 11, 1994. It is not a day-by-day diary of events, but rather a personal account of the highlights of those days, and a commentary of those miles, as I experienced them.

It was a spiritual walk; an American Indian Movement walk to bring attention to Leonard Peltier's case. To put the spotlight back on his unjust conviction of killing two FBI agents eighteen years earlier. Spearheaded by Dennis Banks and his sister, Mary Jane Wilson, the walk would be for 3,800 miles from San Francisco, California, to Washington, D.C., as we tried to bring awareness again on all of the injustices surrounding this case. This was also a spiritual walk to bring attention to other indigenous matters. But above all, we wanted to make the public aware of Leonard Peltier's plight.

On February 11, 1994, Dennis Banks, myself, and about 400 members of the American Indian Movement started the morning by taking the ferryboats out to Alcatraz Island. We loaded everyone, and our sacred drums, onto three ferryboats. A large crowd had gathered to see the "Walk for Justice" off, including children and people of all ages. We loaded the boats, went to the Island of Alcatraz, and had a very emotional sunrise ceremony.

Floyd Crow Westerman and Dennis Banks spoke to all the people who would be walking. My original intention was to go on the walk for a couple of days, then get back home to Las Vegas. Little did I know just how far I would walk before I was done.

We had a pipe ceremony, and I felt honored that Leonard Peltier's mother was there. She thanked everybody that was walking for the cause, walking for her son's case. It was very emotional to see her standing there holding the pipe, thanking everybody. Right then I changed my goal from walking for a few days, and decided, two weeks. I'll go for two weeks.

As I stood there waiting for the Sacred Pipe to work its way around to me, I took the opportunity to study the other peoples faces. I don't think I have ever seen such intensity and emotions radiating from all these serious faces around the circle. It made me proud to be Native and to be able to call these people my friends. An emotional lump worked its way into my throat and I guess something must have gotten into my eyes, they both blured for a minute. I was thinking of all the years Peltier had been away from his family.

'This one's for you brother', I thought as I sent a silent prayer to the Creator for Leonard. The smoke from the Sacred Pipe slowly drifted upwards from my mouth and the red bowl. It was going to where it would do some good.

Then Dennis made people who were **not** aware of Leonard Peltier, listen to the details of his case. He explained what the case involved, and after some sacred words, he passed the pipe to each person who was going on the walk.

They started to play the AIM song, and this made everyone there very emotional. It was a very spiritual, moving ceremony, and I felt my own emotions stirring. I knew once I smoked the pipe I was committed to carry out my pledge to walk. I would walk to correct an injustice. I knew in my heart and in my mind that I was ready, and I was anxious to get started.

I had not been able to make the Sundance the year before, and while I smoked the sacred Chanupa, the Creator placed the thought in my mind that I needed to become a Sundancer. I promised Creator that I would Sundance this year, in Minnesota, in August. So every mile I walked, I knew would help me get in shape for the Sundance, and I would be helping out a good cause at the same time. If you don't know what a Sundance is, well it is a spiritual ceremony of sacrifice. We go through four days of dancing in the hot sun, without food or water. Some Sundancers, most of the men pierce their chests and/or backs. You can find out more of what happens and why in Manny Twofeathers book, "Road to the Sundance." It's a hard road to choose, but I felt the Creator wanted me to Sundance.

It truly was a spiritual walk, and tied in with Leonard Peltier's case. It was a good enough reason for me to go as far as I could, not knowing how far that would be. I said to myself, "If I can't walk for two weeks, then I'm not ready for the Sundance". That gave me even more of an incentive to complete my commitment.

We all smoked the pipe, lined up, and shook hands. When the ceremony was over, I made my way to Mrs. Peltier who was talking to Dennis. I thought to myself she looks like an Indian grandmother who should be surrounded by little kids, telling Indian stories of the old ways. Dennis introduced me to her. I told her that Leonard and I worked together in Milwaukee and both of us were present at the B.I.A. takeover. I told her that I knew he was innocent and I wanted to see him get out, so we hoped this walk would be a success. She asked where I was from and what tribe I was a member of. After some small talk she asked if I was going to walk the entire distance to Washington, D.C. I told her I was not sure how much time I would be able to spend, but that I was in full support of the walk and Leonard's plight. I gave her a hug, and she became very emotional, which touched me deeply.

After composing herself, she thanked Dennis and I saying, "I hope that this walk for justice will bring my Leonard home."

Walking away, I was building up to a quiet rage. I was thinking, here is a man who had been imprisoned for 18 years for something he did not do, deprived of his freedom and the time to spend with his mother and family to live a normal life. I thought to myself, "it's the same, old American justice at work, only in modern times." I was ready to get off Alcatraz and start walking and making some noise, "Wake up America, before it is too late!"

After everybody shook hands with Leonard Peltier's mother, Dennis Banks gave a speech to explain the reason we had the sunrise ceremony here.

Alcatraz Island was originally occupied by the military from the 1850's to 1933 and had served as a post protecting the Bay shoreline, during the Spanish-American War. It was used as disciplinary barracks. After the military vacated in 1933 Alcatraz was turned into a maximum-security prison.

The first 20 Indian prisoners were Hopi elders who refused to send their children to boarding schools set up by the government. The elders were sent to Alcatraz to keep them away from their people, so the other members of the tribe would conform to the government's wishes. The elders were imprisoned for 2 years and after missing their families, agreed to send their children to the schools. Then they were released.

Dennis Banks said that the sunrise ceremony was held on Alcatraz Island to remind us all of the hardships that was bestowed on our Indian brothers and sisters and to take their spirits with us on the walk.

Looking back, I remember all the different things I had heard and all the movies I had seen, about gangsters who were imprisoned on the infamous Alcatraz Island. Now, I find myself standing here with four hundred other Indians, at a Sunrise Ceremony, and I can sense the presence of the warrior spirits who were imprisoned here. I felt sorry for my ancestors who were forced to spend time here. I couldn't help thinking that it really must have been miserable to be here for any reason. I stood there for a moment and thought, "So this is good old Alcatraz Island." It really was a run-down, dark, and ghostly looking place.

The ceremony lasted about two hours, and then everybody filed back out onto the boat ramp where they loaded back onto the ferries, with the sacred Chanupa and the drums.

As the water slapped at the sides of the ferry I feel the wind in my hair. Its good to be here. I turn and look back at Alcatraz Island and a large fog bank is rolling over it. A thought crosses my mind, it had helped us start our journey and now it wanted to cover its shameful past from us.

We had a drum ceremony going back from Alcatraz Island to the port in San Francisco.

Though the sun was high by now there is still a little chill in the air. It feels good. I know that in the days to come we will wish and pray for some cool weather as we move further east and away from the coast. Now we are happy and full of enthusiasum.

It was about a twenty-minute ride back to the mainland where there were news reporters and other people to see us off. We set the drum up in the parking lot and began singing sacred songs to the Creator. A big crowd of people started gathering around.

Off to the side, I was standing there when a young woman I didn't know, came up to me and asked, "What's going on here?" I went into detail, explaining that about seventy of the people here were getting ready to walk to Washington D.C. on "The Walk for Justice". She seemed very interested, and I asked her where she was from. She told me that she was from Sweden and had only been in the United States for a few days. She was interested in how she could join us on this walk. I told her all races of people from all walks of life were welcome. We already had people from Canada, Japan, Australia ... from all over. "Only thing you have to bring is your legs", and I started laughing. I told her we also had a Buddhist Monk named "Junsong" on the walk, he was a non-violent activist.

Dennis told everybody that was going to walk, to gather up and fall into formation. He was making everybody aware of what was going to happen on the first day of the walk. He told us that we would be taking Highway 50 all the way across the United States, from coast to coast. The first day of the walk would cover twenty-five miles. Dennis Banks then handed me the Staff, which is very sacred to the American Indian. You could say that the Staff is to an Indian person what the Rosary is to a Catholic person. I would be carrying one of two Staffs across the U.S. It had twelve eagle feathers and four different colored ribbons on it. The ribbons symbolized the different races. We had a white ribbon for the white race, yellow for the asian race, black for the black race, and red for the red race. That meant that this was a walk for all peoples. **First,** it was an American Indian walk, a walk to bring attention to American Indian problems, but people of all races and religions were invited to join in; for a day, a mile, or whatever length of time or distance they wanted to contribute to the cause.

By now everybody was anxious to start walking, so from San Francisco Bay we began to walk east into the rising sun, starting the five month, 3,800 mile "Walk for Justice" to D.C.

Athough by now I had been up several hours, I felt strange taking the first steps of this journey. It felt like my leg muscles were feeling young and energetic. They were bouncy and stretching to the fullest. Within a matter of a few yards I was in full stride. I was on my path.

As we began our walk down the street, people passing by didn't know what was going on, but they looked and beeped their horns in a friendly way anyway. We were told to walk at a moderate pace, because, after all, we had to cover twenty-five miles.

I felt very honored to be carrying the Sacred

I felt very honored to be carrying the Sacred Staff. The Staff was made by Indian brothers who were prisoners in San Quentin, who had asked Dennis Banks on one of his visits, if they made a Staff for the Walk for Justice, would we carry it for them from coast to coast. Dennis Banks agreed to do it. That was the Staff that I was carrying, and I felt very honored to be carrying it. So with the two Staffs, the American Indian flag, and "Free Leonard Peltier" banners scattered among the seventy people, our walk was underway.

Carrying the Sacred Staff meant I was always at the front. No one was allowed, at any time, to pass in front of the Staff because of what it represented. From the beginning of the walk I was always at the front, carrying the Staff. I felt a strong sense of pride, knowing I had the Staff in my possession. It gave me a sense of power. It gave me inner and outer strength. I knew that with the energies I felt coming from the Staff I would have the commitment to walk my walk and get where the Creator was leading me to go. I had these feelings only five minutes into the walk.

At that point I didn't know what to expect. But I knew that this wasn't going to be your old everyday walk in the park. We were all playing a very important part in Indian history. We were walking for executive clemency to free Leonard Peltier, who had, to date, been imprisoned for eighteen years.

We were also walking to present fifteen conditions; fifteen wrongs inflicted on native peoples, to Congress at the conclusion of the Walk for Justice. These fifteen conditions were:

1. Executive clemency for imprisoned AIM leader Leonard Peltier.
2. The return of the Sacred Black Hills, Paha Sapa, to the Lakota Nation.
3. The restoration of title and deed to 2.9 million acres of land to the Northern Ute Tribe.
4. The protection and preservation of Mount Graham and other spiritual sites.
5. Stoppage of mining on the Black Mesa.
6. The ban of nuclear testing or storage on Western Shoshone land.
7. The full recognition of Anishnabe Ojibway Treaty rights.
8. The halting of federal subsidies to schools using racial logos and mascots.
9. Human rights and spiritual freedom granted to native prisoners.
10. Stoppage of nuclear dumping on native lands.
11. Federal enforcement to stop desecration of grave sites.
12. Taking a stand against hydro genetics in Quebec.
13. The revocation of NAFTA.
14. The suspension of GATT sanctions against Mexico.
15. The closing of the school of American Training for Representatives in the military.

For those not familiar with Leonard Peltier's case, Leonard Peltier is a Lakota Ojibwa who was arrested by Federal marshals. He was accused of killing two FBI agents in a nine-hour gun battle that took place on June 6, 1975 at the Jumping Bull Ranch near Oglala, South Dakota, on the Pine Ridge Reservation. Peltier was tried in federal court in Custer, South Dakota. (How appropriate a city for the trial of an Indian!) He was found guilty and sentenced to two consecutive life terms. Two other men involved in the firefight with Peltier were charged. They were tried in a federal court in Cedar Rapids, Iowa on the same charges, but found not guilty due to justifiable self-defense.

Eighteen years after the Peltier conviction, U.S. Prosecutor Len Cook admitted to a reviewing court, "We don't know who killed the agents." The U.S. parole board refused to consider Peltier's request for parole and will not take any further action in the case until the year 2008. Furthermore, all of Leonard Peltier's avenues of release have been exhausted, and the only way he can get out of prison now is through executive clemency. The only person that can give him executive clemency is the President, so the Walk for Justice focused on getting President Clinton to take notice of the case and give him executive clemency. Hopefully President Clinton will be sympathetic because of what's been done to Leonard Peltier.

Putting this all into perspective, the Walk was planned, put together, and took place, all to bring attention to his case. Therefore, it truly was the "Walk for Justice."

Getting back to when we took off from the San Francisco area, it was a real sunny day. Everybody was in good spirits and full of energy. I started thinking to myself, "This is what I want to do. This is what I really want." I put all my energy reserves on go and stepped along proudly, with a purpose to each step. That's what we all started doing as we headed for our first stop. That would be Sacramento, at the campus where Dennis Banks would be giving a speech and lecture on what the Walk for Justice was all about. He would talk about Leonard Peltier, and he would talk about the other reasons why we were walking.

Well, this is going to be an interesting day, I thought. I had not walked more than a mile in the last two or three years. Back in good old Las Vegas, having two vehicles, I did not **have** to walk, and I was not used to walking very far. I was curious about how well my feet were going to hold up.

Back in the group I could see people of various ages, from thirteen to sixty. For forty-two years old I felt that I was in pretty good shape, but I would have to check and see if I still felt that way at the end of the day. I said to myself, "This is important. This is the time. It's now or never."

We had to walk through the city for fifteen miles or so until we got to Highway 50. People were driving by, beeping and hollering, giving us a variety of signs and symbols, and they were all good. Some were saying, "Yeah, free Leonard Peltier," and various others were throwing in their own remarks. When we got out of the city onto Highway 50, the Highway Patrol came up to us. The officers said that we couldn't walk on Highway 50 because it wasn't safe. Dennis Banks pulled up in a support vehicle and asked them what the problem was. He told them we had a permit to walk on Highway 50, and he produced the permit. The Highway Patrol said that that was all fine and dandy, but there was a lot of construction taking place on this particular part of the road, and it was too narrow and unsafe for pedestrians.

In order for us to get where we were going we had to detour. After taking this detour we would come back out to Highway 50. To avoid the hassle and confrontation with the Highway Patrol we went twenty miles out of our way the very first day. We weren't obligated to do that, but in a very kind way it was **suggested** we take an alternate route. This would make the first day of our walk **45** miles instead of 25.

Dennis Banks decided to have the group take this detour, and finally, at about nine o'clock at night, we came into the little town and found the church that was going to put us up for the night. Everybody was tired, hungry, and had sore feet, and it was only the very first day of walking. We had been walking for over **ten hours**. The whole group consisted of fifty to sixty people, and you could read the pain on everyone's face after finishing about forty-five miles.

Dennis Banks told us that it was going to be a custom at the end of each day to form a circle and have a ceremony to close the day out. Sage is very sacred to the American Indian, and each person on the Walk would stand there in the circle as a guide, or one of the walkers, came around with a bucket containing sage that was smoldering. Everybody would sage themselves by fanning the smoke toward their body. It was a blessing, a way to finish the day in a good way, a way to give thanks for making it through the day. So at the end of each day we saged ourselves down and had a closing drum ceremony.

As tired as everybody was, this would go on, sometimes for ten or fifteen minutes. We welcomed this ceremony, even if it meant we had to stand a little bit longer, because we were saging off and thanking Creator for the safe completion of the day.

We would rest for the night, and everyone had their own way of relaxing. Some would read, others would play chess or checkers, and some would go into the nearest town and get a good old Big Mac or Whopper, or whatever . . . or just do some shopping.

So, we pretty much got into a routine on the very first day: We would walk from eight o'clock in the morning to five o'clock at night. We had the hours after five o'clock at night to do whatever we wanted. If you felt like you wanted to go to sleep right away, or you had to write a letter, or whatever, that was your own free time.

On the first day I was quick to find the nearest telephone so I could call my wife and tell her how the day went. I quickly earned the distinction of being the person to find a telephone anywhere it could be found.

Later on in the trip they would say, "If you're looking for Kindness, look for the nearest telephone and you'll find him." And, my phone bills at home would prove that. After the phone call to my wife I found my gear in the support vehicle which was carrying all our backpacks. At that point I could think of only one thing—going to sleep. I found myself a comfortable little spot under a big table in the church basement. I got out of my clothing, took a hot shower, and the next thing I knew I fell asleep.

In no time at all, it seemed, I heard somebody say "Everybody up! Everybody up! Where do you people think you are, a Holiday Inn?" This person, we soon found out, was Rooster; a full blooded Lakota Sioux, who was known for being able to get people up and going with his jokes, pranks, and most of all, his bullhorn. I mean, the last thing I wanted to hear in the morning was a bullhorn loudspeaker blaring "Get up! Get up!" But, that's the way it went. Everybody loved to "hate" Rooster.

Everybody got up with sore feet and sore legs, knowing that today, the second day, we **only** had to walk twenty-five miles. The group got their backpacks rolled, took care of their bathroom duties, and a minister and his wife gave us pancakes, bacon, and eggs for breakfast. All the people in the church congregation had come in early and made breakfast for the Walk for Justice. These were just the first of some very nice people that we would meet on the Walk, people who really cared and did their best to take good care of us.

The first thing we did to start the day was called The Circle. Here, everybody would meet in the morning at The Circle and sage off to start the day, just like we would at the end of each night. Dennis Banks would talk to the walkers and explain to them how far we had to walk, and what was on the agenda for the day. He'd also tell us where we possibly might be staying that night. Everybody had to be up and ready. If you weren't up and ready or they couldn't get you up for some reason, it was up to you to catch up to the walkers, whether they were five miles down the road or two miles down the road. Now and then we would have an occasional walker that would have to catch up, but everyone was always able to link back up with the rest of the walkers.

There is only one Highway 50 that goes from coast to coast, and it's not like you have to go through a whole lot of unnecessary trouble to find it. It was there every morning, staring all of us in the face. We had three support vehicles that carried all the backpacks, food, donations, camping equipment, tents, and everything else. If we hadn't had the support vehicles we would have been carrying backpacks. But, thanks to those who had donated the trucks and support vehicles, we were able to have our camping equipment moved to and from our camping spots without us having to carry it. It was a great relief to us to know that everything was being carried in the vehicles, and all **we** had to do was get through the miles, carry our own selves down the road, and put more miles under our belts, without having to carry a back pack.

Speaking of a great relief, on the second day of walking we were fortunate enough to be put up in another church. It was as comfortable as the night before and we were treated just as well. They found space for everyone to sleep in this church and it was great. Everybody was happy, including me, that we didn't have to pitch our tents, because the farther east we went, the colder it got. In just 60 miles, and two days of walking, the nights were getting real cold. We knew that sooner or later, we would have to camp out. Little did we know that it would come upon us only a day later, when we would have to make camp and sleep in a state park. Everybody had to pitch a tent, which wasn't too bad because the sun was just setting, and it was really pristine and beautiful country up in the Sierras. Nobody really minded.

We had picked up additional walkers in Sacramento, and it was on to Placerville. We stayed at a campsite that was just a total nightmare for me. I mean, I hate cold, and it was all day walking in the cold, and setting up our tents in the cold. With me being the city boy from Vegas, I was not too happy about this **at all**. I questioned myself saying, "What the hell are you doing here, man?" But, I knew the reason. All I had to do was think of Leonard and how he might be feeling. That mattered a whole lot more than my being cold, so I just put it in the back of my mind and went on with what I had to do.

That particular night it had dropped down below zero; bone chilling cold. I had all the proper equipment in case I had to handle this situation, but I'm not a person that enjoys cold weather at all, so it was hard on me. We got through that night with our tents covered with snow. What irritated me even more was that we had to walk in the cold all day, had to set our tents up in the cold, and then had to get up and start the next day in the cold. It really was hard for me to get started. I said to myself "The sooner I get started, the sooner I'll get warm". It was real rough going for all of us, but we got back on track and headed east toward good, old Lake Tahoe.

It warmed up after everybody broke down their tents and set off on the road to Tahoe. I said to myself, "What do I have to complain about? I might be cold, but I'm healthy." Then I got to thinking about Leonard Peltier. He's been locked up in a 9' x 5' cell for the last eighteen, going on nineteen, years. He would welcome this cold. He would welcome this freedom. He would love to be in my shoes. I'm a free man and I'm healthy. My fellow walkers and I were in good spirits. What did we have to complain about? So, I left it at that in my mind and continued to walk, warming my body by putting more miles under my belt.

Personally I couldn't even tell you what I saw the first two hundred miles of the Walk. I was trying to adjust my mind and get used to it by turning myself into a walking machine. I had to block out my past life in Las Vegas and what I could be doing. I had to think, "Hey, I'm here now, so deal with it". I would be lying if I said there weren't times in the first two hundred miles when I said to myself, "Man do you know what you got yourself into?" Knowing that Creator would get me through this spiritual walk, I just decided to put it in His hands, quit my bitching, and continue to do what I had to do.

By now we were up in the rocky and hilly mountain range of the Sierras. It is very beautiful country going towards Lake Tahoe, and the weather was quite comfortable for walking during the day- despite the up and down of the terrain. But, it was still pretty hard on the feet and the back. It was not, by any means, a cakewalk.

We had people on the walk who would say, "Kindness, can we have a smoke break? Can I stop and take a stone out of my shoe?" We had our various breaks and water stops, but we had to stay on a specific timetable as far as the pace we had to keep. We had support vehicles behind us as we walked to the side of the white line. We would come to areas every once-in-a-while where there wasn't even a white line. At that point Dennis Banks said that for the walkers' safety we would have a station wagon follow the end of the line with a banner on the back saying, "Caution - Walkers Ahead." We wanted this walk to be accident free and as comfortable as we could make it for everybody. We did that to the best of our ability, and tried to keep it that way throughout the duration of the walk.

Everybody would be talking with each other, chatting and singing, whistling or whatever, and sometimes they wouldn't pay attention to how far out in the road they were. It was up to me to turn around and see that the formation stayed "Tight and Right", so there wouldn't be any accidents.

NEVADA

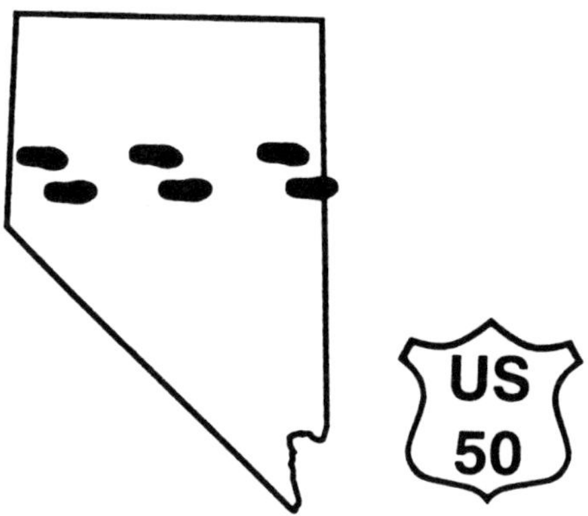

Five days after leaving the San Francisco Bay area, on February 16th, 1994, we were at the state line of California and Nevada. We had finally walked to Lake Tahoe. Everyone was happy to be there. It was just a little closer to Washington, D.C. - five days closer. I was just happy to be that much closer to D.C., in the land of Lake Tahoe, Nevada. It made me feel closer to my wife back home, and kept me from feeling so homesick. Being in my own home state felt good.

All the walkers were put up in one of the local high school gyms. Sleeping in the school gymnasium was as good as being in a house after spending three days out in the cold in a tent. This would be our first day off from walking and we could spend it doing whatever we wanted to do.

I had some extra lucky Indian coins in my pocket and I wanted to go to a Casino. I had intentions of spending only five dollars, but I ended up spending forty. This really got to me because this was money I had to live on, and I **knew** better. So I thought, "Well, that's what I get for going to a Casino when I know better." So I told myself that's it, I'm going to stay the hell out of the Casinos the rest of my time here. That would be about eighteen more hours. I left it at that.

Naturally, I lived up to my reputation and found a telephone that was only a stone's throw away. I had to call my wife and let her know how the last five days had gone. She was still excited about it all, and she marked her map with a yellow marker to keep track of us from county to county and state to state. She had to hold down the fort back in Las Vegas and couldn't be with me. Following where I was on the map made her feel closer to me.

She was definitely going to get the scoop on the three cold days and the last two good days I had walked. We had a great conversation, and, of course, I told her that I missed her and I loved her. I also told her to relay a message to my brother Dale. He was really interested in following the walk, too. I asked her to tell everyone in the family that I loved them and I would talk to her again tomorrow. That was the extent of the conversation, but not the extent of how much I missed her.

Even though I lived in Nevada, I had never been to Lake Tahoe. I took the day to look around at the different shops, but my main thing was to get a nice card, go to the post office, and mail it off. I was just checking off all the little things I had to do, glad that I wasn't on a schedule. It was just kind of a mental relief to know I had the day to do whatever I wanted.

After being in the city for awhile, I almost forgot I had been out on the road walking for five days. I thought that this was funny. After I bought and wrote out a card I asked a guy where the post office was. He said it was about a mile and a half down the way, and said I could catch a bus over there. I'm thinking, you mean to tell me I just walked over a hundred miles and I'm going to get on the bus to mail this postcard to my wife! I don't think so! I thought, "Hey, I can walk that in a minute." So, I walked to the post office and took care of my business, then found my way back to the high school, and went to sleep.

The next morning I had to contend with old Rooster, his bullhorn, and his usual way of waking everybody up: "Cock-a-doodle-do, where do think you are, at the Holiday Inn? This is the Walk for Justice and we've got over three thousand miles to go yet. Get your lazy butts up." You could hear laughing from various sleeping bags and tents. Everybody had grown accustomed to his insults. I think that secretly we kind of liked them. He had everybody going. You know, everybody was up and at 'em to start the next day and raring to get some more miles under our belts. So, we all got together at the circle and had the sunrise ceremony. Everybody saged off and thanked the people and the superintendent of the school for letting us stay the night. It really was a great comfort to be there, even sleeping on a hardwood floor in a sleeping bag. We put our gear away on the vehicles and left the gym, continuing on our walk toward D.C.

Leaving the Tahoe area, we walked down through the main strip. People were looking out of casinos' windows and wondering what was going on. There was a lot of oohing and ahhing, as if to say they were surprised about us being there. Some people were coming out asking if we were the Indian people that were walking across the U.S.A. My comment was "Yeah, you're right, that's us. This is the walk to help Leonard Peltier get out of prison." People were giving their comments, most agreeing that he was unjustly convicted, but some had different opinions.

After getting past the curious onlookers, we had to wait for the light at the intersection. I glanced over and looked at the paper box and saw the headlines of the Tahoe Daily Tribune: "Indians on Walk for Justice Cross Country. Walkers pass though Tahoe." I said to the guy walking behind me, "Yo! We finally got some news coverage. Somebody fall back and pick up a newspaper or two so we can see what they got to say about us."

About that time, Bruce Johnson fell back and picked one up. He ran back and caught up with the walkers. He said he would put it away and we would read it later to see what they had to say. It made me feel pretty good that we were finally getting some notice. With what we were doing, it was a good feeling to know that somebody was printing information about the walk. It really made my day and put a little more pep in my step.

We had one state under our belts. That was a good feeling too, especially when you considered the Sierra Nevada Mountain area we had just covered. There were jokes and talk going around, all about the famous, "Highway 50, the loneliest road in the world". It has that reputation, and as we traveled across the whole state of Nevada we would find out that it was well deserved. It wasn't going to be any little short walk. And it wasn't going to be a very pleasant one, either.

Highway 50 goes through Shoshone Territory, and we were told that we would be spending some time on the Shoshone Reservation. It is nothing but totally flat, and that would be the reverse of what we just went through. It would also be windy and cold. I was looking forward to camping at the Shoshone Reservation for the simple fact that I had never met any one from the Shoshone Tribe. I was really excited about staying with these Indian people on their reservation. A car pulled up along side me and asked if this was Walk for Justice. I told them yes, it sure was. I could see that the people in the car were Indian. It turned out that they were from the Shoshone Tribe. They joined us on the Walk.

Walking seemed to take forever. We finally got into the town of Fallon, Nevada, where the Shoshone Tribe would be welcoming us. We were all very tired and glad to see the gymnasium off in the distance. It looked just as good as a Holiday Inn. We were really happy to be reaching that destination. The land was flat and we could see the gymnasium from the highway because it was the only thing out there.

The closer we got, I thought my ears were playing tricks on me. When we got within a mile or so, I could hear drumming. It wasn't a real cold day, but quite windy, and I could hear the pounding of the drums being carried on the wind. When we got closer we could see a group of Indian drummers in the parking lot in front of the gymnasium, welcoming us with a drum ceremony. It warmed my heart to hear those drums, and I thanked Creator for getting us to that point, and keeping all of us safe.

When we arrived we formed a circle and everybody saged off. People from the Shoshone Tribe joined in the circle and shook hands with each and every one of the walkers, thanking us for the miles covered and for what we were doing. They were very proud to have us stay with them for the four-day break that we would be taking. There would be a long rest, festivities, and a feast. We enjoyed four days of pow wow, drumming, music, and Indian dancing. We were invited to attend it all. We enjoyed this time immensely.

Most of my free time was spent meeting new people and making friends with the Shoshones. I went into Carson City to visit the Stewart Indian Museum and really enjoyed that. It helped me to learn more about the Shoshone people. I did all the things I wasn't able to do in the days that we were walking. I sent postcards, laid back, put my feet up, and found out what it meant to totally relax. The rest was well deserved by everyone.

I met some Shoshone people that invited all the walkers out to a medicinal sweat lodge. Five other walkers and myself went to this sweat, along with some of the Shoshones. There were about twelve of us, and it was rumored that there was going to be one hundred and thirty rocks in the center of this Sweat Lodge. I was surprised they were using that many rocks. Most I've ever had in a sweat was fifty to sixty rocks. I was eager to go and see how different it would be, but I was also hesitant. We went out to the guy's house who was having the sweat. His name was Otis, and he was a full-blooded Shoshone. He would later become good friends with me, and would join us on the walk for over a month.

We had a phenomenal sweat. We were in that Sweat Lodge for two hours with no water breaks. The prayers they had to say for themselves and the rest of the walkers were so good I didn't even miss the water. This I do know, the stones were blue - that's how hot they were. Every time a rock came in we just looked at each other like, oh, this is going to be hot. It was a very hot sweat, but I owed it to myself to finish. The Creator helped me get through it, and it was a very spiritual sweat. It also helped to strengthen me for the upcoming months. I needed to be strong for the sweats I would be enduring for the purification before Sundancing, and the sweats we had going across the country helped me. They gave me a spiritual lift, because those Indian brothers know about the sweat, and know it's a very religious ceremony. It helps you in many different ways when you're praying. It helps you to be strong and it did help me on the Walk for Justice.

After that sweat, I felt like a huge weight had been lifted off my back and my muscles and bones felt relieved. We had a feast and I thanked Otis, as did the rest of the Indian brothers. I thanked him with a hug and some tobacco. I could tell by the look in his eyes that it was appreciated and could be of some help. As we were getting ready to go back to camp Otis said to me, after knowing me for less than three hours, "I want to give you a gift to add to the Staff you are carrying." To my surprise and honor, he handed me two eagle feathers. I thanked him and said I would definitely have to put them on the staff first thing in the morning. "Thanks brother for the eagle feathers and the sweat."

It bears mentioning how sacred and important it is to receive eagle feathers to an Indian. If an Indian gives another Indian an eagle feather they are trusting that person with a very sacred object. The eagle flies the highest and is considered closest to the Creator. We believe the eagle carries our prayers to the Creator. Therefore eagle feathers have touched the Creator. So receiving one is a deep and sacred honor.

With that, we all piled back into the Indian van. For those who don't know what an Indian van looks like, it barely rolls down the road, and it's held together with chicken wire. That's just a joke among other Indians. We went back to the campsite where

Dennis Banks and everybody else was having a drum ceremony. He was telling everybody we would be breaking camp and leaving the Shoshone in the morning. Anyone that wanted to join the walk for a mile, a day, or a week was more than welcome. (We would bring five new walkers with us from the reservation, including Otis.)

After that refreshing, religious sweat I climbed into my sleeping bag, knowing we would be back to walking that road in the morning after our sunrise ceremony. We would all be walking the walk for Leonard Peltier and all other indigenous matters. We would be bringing up these issues with the Congress in Washington, D.C. With that on my mind, I went to sleep.

The next morning we broke camp and had a drum ceremony. The Shoshone sent us off, and we had other Shoshone people that took the day off to walk with us until we got off the reservation. We welcomed that. It felt good to look back and see we had about a hundred and fifty people walking with the American Indian flag, "Free Leonard Peltier" banners and the two Staffs. It was inspiring to see many Indian brothers and sisters and all the other walkers and supporters — black, white, Japanese, people from Germany, all races. We had a whole collage of races there, and people could see that we were united as one, as we walked down the road. People were stopping, beeping and screaming good things about the Walk for Justice. Throughout the day, kids from ages ten to fourteen, and parents walked with us. That really amazed me. Not once did I hear anyone say they were tired.

We got to the point where they would leave us. We all took a ten-minute break, thanked everyone for walking with us, and said our good-byes. We gave our handshakes and hugs and they got into the vans that drove out to pick them up. I took one last glance back to hear the beeps and see the waves, not knowing if I would ever see any of these people again. I felt a loss, like those were people that I had known for a long time, not just four days. Keeping my emotions in check I put them into my steps, wondering if it would get better or worse, and just continued walking.

We got out of Fallon and hit the main stretch of Highway 50 that goes straight across Nevada. I could see why they called it the loneliest highway in the world. As far as the eye could see there was blacktop, flatness, some scrub brush, and nothing else. I commented to Bruce, who was behind me, "Talk about nothing? There's nothing as far as the eye can see." There was nothing in front of us but flat desert.

It would take us three and a half weeks to cross this lonely stretch of Nevada; a total of 407 miles across the famous, loneliest road, Highway 50. I found this to be the hardest part of the trip, these three and a half weeks. The road lived up to its reputation as far as I was concerned, because it was almost like walking with blinders on. There was nothing to the right and nothing to the left, just one long, black road. I thanked the Creator for a particular individual named Barry War bonnet, a Lakota Sioux that was on the walk. He was the other Staff carrier. He would drum traditional Lakota songs while we were walking, and everybody would join in and try to pick up the words and learn the song. By the time we were midway through that 407 miles, many people could sing the songs. They were difficult if you never spoke the Lakota language before. We entertained ourselves, and kept from going crazy, by singing these Lakota songs as we walked through the heat waves of the day.

The weather was good during the day and the exact opposite during the night. We would try to be at a campsite and have all of our tents pitched by five, because it turned cold after that. Not being very fond of the cold, I would be one of the first people to have my tent pitched so I could get in my insulated sleeping bag. The quicker I got in there, the warmer and better I felt. Sometimes at the end of the day, my feet and I were so tired. All the other walkers felt the same way, I'm sure. I would climb into my tent and get into my sleeping bag — clothes, shoes and all. That's all I would remember.

I would be out for the count till the next morning, when I would hear good old Rooster and his wake-up call. This was funny to some and not so funny to others. Personally, I loved to joke around and really enjoyed Rooster's joking ways. I learned to grow quite fond of him by the time the trip was over.

It was now March 11th, and it had been one month since we had left Alcatraz Island in San Francisco. In that month's time I had made friends, become closer to some of the other walkers, and really got to know some good people. We had fallen into a routine. We were a pretty good whole body, whole unit, because we all knew what we had to do from sun-up to sundown.

At this time, I felt like we were finally starting to get organized. We now had an official cook that had joined on, and the food was getting better, which improved people's morale. We never had much to complain about as far as food. The meals were always there. A good breakfast every day, sometimes no lunch, but always a good supper. After mealtime, we fell into a routine where everyone was doing what they wanted to do. We had drum ceremonies, we sang, and we gossiped. Some people worked on making drums and other crafts with their free time. Everybody was doing their own thing and had time to chat around. We became our own little community at night, after the walking was over for the day. It was a social time to do whatever you wanted to do.

I spent my free time laying in my tent, writing letters back to my wife and family. I wished I had a good old cellular phone so I could be in contact with my wife and other people I know. Knowing that wasn't possible, I just took it in stride. Out on Highway 50 there were no telephones, no Seven-Eleven's, no McDonald's – nothing! It was just Highway 50 and nothing else besides wildlife and occasional birds of prey for the wildlife that wasn't fast enough. I saw various forms of wildlife that I normally wouldn't be able to see if I hadn't been on the walk, and I enjoyed it very much.

What I didn't enjoy was the road-kill for the people on the walk who had weak stomachs — not me though. I became known as somewhat of a character. I would laugh it off whenever I would see some gross road kill. I would bring it to the women's attention because I knew I could get a good laugh out of it. Besides that, you could smell the road kill before you could even see it. I would say, "there's road kill comin' up. I smell it . . . Road kill comin' up, don't step on it." Over the miles it got to be nothing, and the women got to joking around about it as much as I did. In fact, I overheard one woman say, "Road kill comin' up. It sort of reminds me of some body. Yeah, it looks like my ex!" At that point, everybody in the formation started laughing. There was always something going on in a joking way. Everybody learned to accept it whether it was in good taste or bad. We were just having fun, making jokes, and that helped to break up the boredom. It kept us from getting hypnotized from the long, black, lonely road . . . Highway 50.

My only good thought then, was that we were going through Nevada and crossing Highway 50 in the winter. Rumor had it that it could get up to 130 degrees out here. This is the road you do not cross without having water in your radiator and your car in good shape. Also, you need extra water in your trunk. People have been known to get out on this road and die in their cars. They died of thirst, or had near death experiences, underestimating this road in the summer time.

In the days it took to get across the four hundred and seven-mile stretch, there would sometimes be hours when we wouldn't see a vehicle coming or going in either direction. I said to myself, Man what would you do if you got stuck out here." All the time thinking, hey I'm out here by choice, and I'm **walking** it.

The look on the faces of the people, when we did encounter a vehicle, was like, "What the hell?", or "Who are these people walking out here in the middle of nowhere?" They were surprised to see a group of sixty people with a flag and Staffs, in straight formation, walking down the side of Highway 50, in the desolate area where there was <u>nothing</u>. You could see the amazement on their faces as they drove by. I suppose that if it were the other way around **I** would be wondering what the hell these people were doing out here in the middle of Bumf---, Egypt!

We all knew what we were doing out here and why we were on Highway 50. We didn't really care about anybody else's reaction. So what if they wondered what we were doing out in the middle of nowhere. We knew why we were there, and that was a good enough reason for myself and everybody else. We would have an occasional car pull over to the side. They wouldn't know about the Walk for Justice and would ask why we were out there. Somebody would fall back, out of formation, to explain why we were walking, and the reason for walking. Our people would say, "If you're really interested, you'll sign our petition."

We did get signatures all the way across the United States. We got everybody's signature that we talked to that was interested in the cause. We ended up getting 750,000 signatures by the time the walk was over. They came from people we encountered on the way, in towns, and on the road. We would have a seminar at the nearest college campus and set up a booth to make people aware of the reason for the Walk for Justice. We would explain the fifteen reasons we were walking. In addition, we would take donations, and we sold "Walk for Justice" T-shirts and buttons. That would help out with gas money. Many people expressed a great deal of sympathy and support for the cause. We actually lived off money and food donations picked up along the way.

Speaking of donations, when we were about one hundred and fifty miles onto Highway 50 in Nevada and had another two hundred and fifty-seven miles to go, it seemed like we were on a treadmill. It was about our fourth day of walking here, and it was particularly hot for winter. We heard this loud noise. We looked behind us and a semi-truck was barreling down the road. We moved to the side of the road to avoid being hit, and the truck raced by us beeping his horn. Everybody waved and gave him the raised fist salute of AIM. To our amazement, the truck got about one hundred yards past us and slowed to a stop. As we caught up to the truck, a big burly truck driver out of California said, "You're the Indian guys walking across the United States. I heard all about you. Other truckers have seen you and I heard about you guys on my CB. I was hoping I would run into you. I think this is a real great thing you're doing for Leonard Peltier. What the hell's wrong with the FBI anyway? They think they can get away with anything." He was really aware of what went on with Peltier's case and made a big impression on us by knowing the facts.

At that point, he said "Enough chit-chat", and asked to sign our petition. He signed the petition and walked up to the back of his truck. He opened one of the doors and put four cases of cold oranges down on the blacktop and said, "Hey, you didn't see me do this. Good luck to you guys." He gave a wave, climbed back up into his cab, and took off. We were all real surprised and grateful that he was the person he was.

One of the support vehicles that was about a half mile behind us had come up to see why we had stopped, and we said "This is the reason why". They loaded those fresh, cold oranges in the support vehicle and that night we had somewhat of an orange feast. We enjoyed them to the full extent.

After walking all day for 30 miles, we pulled in midway between Fallon and Austin, Nevada and made camp. Everybody was pitching their tents and watching while a beautiful, red, desert sunset was taking place. A lot of people stopped to take pictures.

A Mountain Ranger pulled up in his vehicle and told us that he was aware that the Walk for Justice was going to be camping off to the side of the road. He came out to warn us to sleep in a tight circle because there were a lot of mountain lions in the area, and they didn't want anyone to get bitten or eaten. Dennis

Banks thanked him for giving us the information, and everybody put their tents back to back and shoulder to shoulder in a complete circle, with the support vehicles around it. We joked and said that it was something we had learned from the white man. We had two or three extra fires going. I wasn't about to get bitten or eaten by a mountain lion. Although we knew the chances of that happening were next to nothing, everybody, including myself, was still spooked. I remember going to bed that night and not sleeping very solid after hearing the warning from the Ranger. As spooked as I was, I eventually did fall asleep and woke up happy that no one had been eaten, and ready to go the next morning. When I woke up, a lady was outside my tent, looking around in the sand. When I asked her what she was looking for, she said "Mountain lion tracks. I could have sworn I heard one". I said "Yea, right". She started laughing and let me know she was only joking.

After breakfast we saged off, and Dennis Banks made everybody aware of what was going to go on that day. We found out it was the birthday of one of the girls from Japan. Dennis and I had everyone sing happy birthday to her, and then we began our walk, back on good old Highway 50 again. We started the day out, one foot in front of the other. We had a lot of sore feet and there were people who weren't able to continue walking. For one day they had to ride in the support vehicle. There were only two people that decided it was too hard, or they just didn't want to walk any more. Out of those people who started the walk from Alcatraz Island, there were about 12 that remained. The rest we had picked up in Sacramento, Fallon, and our Shoshone brothers and sisters who came from the Reservation. Everybody had sore feet. My feet felt like they were going to burst off my ankles. But the Creator saw to it that I would keep going, and he made me strong. I just kept walking. There was no time to bitch about how sore your feet were. You just bandaged them up with moleskin, kind of forgot about them, and went on.

While we're on the subject of feet, everyone quickly learned the "Do's and Don'ts" of how to keep your feet in good shape. The best way was to put Vaseline on your feet from toes to ankle and wear two pairs of socks. It helped enormously. It's what long distance runners do. The first pair of socks took care of friction so your feet aren't rubbing against your shoes. I had invested in a good pair of German made Lowa boots. I went through three pairs, and after the trip I wound up writing the company to tell them what a great boot they were. They were leather-lined, and that really helped save my feet, compared to what the other walkers were going through. When I went to buy all my equipment, the guy was a great help by telling me about the significance of a good pair of shoes as opposed to putting all your money into equipment. He said if you're going to be walking all that far, whether you have a backpack on or not, you should be putting your money into your boots. With me being a city boy, taking his advice really paid off. After the Walk I went back to the outfitting store where I bought all my equipment and my Lowa boots and really thanked them.

The walk went on through Nevada and things started to get a lot better. This is where we started having a person on the walk, designated as the mail-person, who would pick up everybody's mail at designated mail stops along the route. He had a card issued to him, giving him the authority to pick up the mail. He would not only pick up mail, packages, and other things that people had sent to them; he would also drop off the mail. So I had mail coming in from my wife, my brother, and my family, as various little care packages. It made things a little easier. This mail-person would later become a good friend of mine. His name was Dave Patton, and he was with his wife Linda, and his son. They joined the walk in Sacramento, but I had not become acquainted with them until we were half way through Nevada.

This far into the walk, Barry War bonnet, the Lakota Sioux who was carrying the other Staff, had to leave the walk and go back home to Colorado. After his month of musical and spiritual drumming songs, we all felt a great loss that he was leaving. We were wishing that he didn't have to go. There were people that came on the walk for a day, an hour, or for weeks, but at some point in time along the walk, people did have to leave.

As soon as we got into Nevada I started thinking about going the whole distance - all 3,800 miles. Though I was suffering from blisters on top of blisters, I could heal. Though I was missing my wife more with every mile that I walked, I could go back to her when the Walk was over.

It kept going through my mind that Leonard Peltier had been in a 5' X 9' cell for over eighteen years, and he could not go back <u>anywhere</u> whenever he wanted. He had no freedom. He would be thankful to be able to have these blisters from walking. He would be thankful to be here, even on the loneliest highway in the world. I knew Leonard Peltier personally, and I knew that I had to walk all the way to D.C. for him, and for his rights. At that point I realized that I had known for some time that I would go the whole distance. I had to. I also knew that at some point I had to tell my wife.

I was the only person that started from Alcatraz that went the whole distance. I'm proud of that, for the simple fact that, as homesick and as bad as my feet hurt at different times in the different situations, the Creator made me strong. I knew in my heart and mind that I had to cover this whole distance. I had to prove to myself that it could be done. I had to prove to myself that **I** could do it. I would be ready for the Sundance in August, at Pipestone in Minnesota.

I would be lying if I said there weren't times I wanted to leave. But the Creator helped me continue to be strong and walk. Dale VanFleet, a full-blooded Indian from the Mojave Tribe, had joined the walk back in Carson City. I hadn't gotten acquainted with him yet, but we soon became good friends. I found him to be extra strong. He was a different type of person, and I really admired him for his strength and for the fact that he was so outgoing on the walk. He was like me, committed to walk non-stop to get these miles by the wayside and get closer to the business that we had to take care of in D.C. We walked those miles, and I got to know Dale VanFleet, the new Staff carrier. We chatted, and I said to him, "As far as Barry War bonnet leaving, I had plans on leaving also. But now I've got to find a phone, out in the middle of nowhere, and call my wife to let her know that my initial plan to come on the walk for a couple of weeks had changed again."

I was pondering over how I was going to tell her that I was going to be gone for another four and a half months, and wondering how she was going to take it. I didn't want to jeopardize my marriage or get her upset, because initially we had agreed that I would go for two weeks. She didn't want to be alone for all that time. So, now I was walking and thinking about how I was going to break the news to her when I found that first phone. Unfortunately, I found it an hour or so after those thoughts. I found the only phone between Fallon and Austin, Nevada. There was a sign above it that said, "This is the loneliest phone on the loneliest highway in Nevada." How appropriate for what I was about to tell my wife.

I walked back two miles to the phone after we camped, to call my wife and explain to her my reasons for wanting to be on the Walk the whole way. As the phone was ringing, I took a deep breath. When Karen picked up the phone I said, "Hello. How are you doing?" She said, "Hi. I'm doing fine. I miss you."

Just what I needed to hear, right off the bat. I told her I loved her and missed her too, and began telling her how tired I was, and how my feet were hurting. I told her that Leonard Peltier would love to feel the way I feel, and he would welcome the blistered feet from walking, since he could only walk around in his cell. I took another deep breath and told her that I had decided to stay on the walk for the whole distance, the whole time. There was silence, then she said, "I know you have to do this for Leonard, and for yourself, but what about me?" I could tell from the sound of her voice that she wasn't thrilled about my decision, but then I heard her say, "Do what you have to do. Somehow we will make it work."

Words can't express how much those words, **"We will make it work"** meant to me. My wife understood, and she supported me. That was a big load off my mind, and it put some extra pep in my step. Financially it was going to be very difficult. The phone bills alone were $500 to $600 a month. After all, she was the only one holding down a job, paying the bills, and sending care packages and money to me on the road. It was tough on her, and there were many trips to the pawnshop when money got tight, and many times when she had to beat the check to the bank. But she saw how important this cause was to me, and she supported me.

Only the Creator can know why I was so blessed to have her by my side. I love her, and felt very lucky to have her support. Although she wasn't very happy at first, she understood, and I greatly appreciated it. It was something that I **had** to do, and she understood that. I was just relieved it hadn't caused any major conflicts between us. It made me feel real good that she understood, and she was with me.

We had mail service for our walkers and I reassured Karen that I would write as often as I could, when I found time, and she said she would write me. At least we had communication by mail if I couldn't get to a phone, and that made us both happy. We figured that that was better than nothing. We got into communicating with each other over the months by mail and phone. It worked out real good for the both of us. As I went back to camp I realized that I was probably the luckiest man alive! Well it felt that way to me.

It seemed like we were on Highway 50 in Nevada forever. We were rapidly approaching our halfway point, which was Austin. Everybody was in good spirits because we knew that we were almost halfway through good old lonely Highway 50, Nevada style. We had been into our walk for roughly an hour when we saw a car approaching. It came to a stop, and in it were two people that were American Indians. They were with the American Indian Movement and they asked where Dennis Banks was. He was back at the camp we had just left, in his trailer. He was making sure that the campground we had left was all clean and tidied up. They thanked us and we continued walking. About 45 minutes later Dennis Banks pulled up in the support vehicle and told the walkers to form a circle towards the east. He said there was a gentleman from the Western Shoshone Tribe, a medicine man by the name of Bear Boy that wanted to wish us a safe journey, say some prayers, and have a pipe ceremony for the walkers. We all formed a circle and this medicine man saged each of the walkers off and sang a prayer song for us that was very moving and emotional.

He said to Dennis Banks that he wanted to walk with us and spend the rest of the day with us so he could say some prayers for us at the end of the day for good health on the rest of the journey across the U.S. We were glad to have this medicine man instill his good wishes and give us the strength to carry us on our journey east.

To this point, all through Sacramento into Reno and Carson City, we had had no trouble or racial problems with anybody. But, on this particular day, we were half the day into our walk, and this pick-up came speeding near the walkers closer than it should have been, and closer than we wanted it to be. Someone yelled racial slurs and gave us the old famous middle finger sign. They made rude comments to us. We all ignored them and did not pay any attention. I said to myself, "Man, out here in the middle of nowhere, walking my ass off, I don't need some stupid rednecks yelling racial insults at myself and the rest of the people." It was almost like I was wishing they would come back and get in my face so I could take out any anger that I had. At the same time, this was a spiritual walk and I didn't want to see that happen, so

I just let it go, and the thoughts quickly left my mind. We continued walking.

Little did I know that this would prepare myself and the rest of the walkers for the upcoming and unnecessary racial comments from various people throughout the different states. However, 90% of the walk was without any racial slurs or comments — except for a few states, which I will get into later. Other than that it went very well, especially considering the fact that we went through 12 different states, from coast to coast. That's all I can really say about anything bad in that sense. We were quite pleased with everything going as well as it did.

Breaking camp in Austin, we had a rather long stretch to our next stop, which would be Eureka. We were looking forward to the next town, and that would make us 80% of the way across Nevada. The closer we were to getting out of Nevada, quite naturally, the closer we were to getting to D.C. You had to be there every day, walking, to know how a mile felt like two miles sometimes, and five miles felt like 20. It just depended on how you felt on any given day. Everybody had their own different way of being moody, and funny, and comical - whatever! Every day was something different.

When we got to the town of Eureka there was a truck stop, and they had a pool table, pinball machines, and a little restaurant. We camped in back of this truck stop and it was really a lot of fun. We spent a good amount of time playing pool and eating what we wanted to eat in this restaurant. Or, if you wanted, you could eat the daily menu that the Walk cook would be making. Dennis Banks would often joke that we would be having the "guess what" plate tonight. That would be the special. For a change I had a nice burger plate, and I enjoyed every bite of it.

The people in the restaurant were quite friendly. I was browsing around looking at souvenirs, and I found one that was a little hatpin. It said on it "I survived the loneliest road. Nevada Highway 50". It had the Highway 50 road sign on it. I thought it was quite appropriate, and for $2.50 you couldn't beat it. I bought that and quickly pinned it on my hat next to my other pin that said Stewart Indian Museum. Carson City, Nevada", another little memento. That was the extent of that night. As I went to bed there was a ceremony going on, thanking Creator for the good day's walk, and for the fact that all the walkers were healthy and in good shape. With that, the drums put me to sleep. I was soon out cold, until the next morning when I heard the Rooster crow — the notorious bullhorn and Rooster crow that everybody had become accustomed to.

Everybody was in exceptionally good spirits that day because we all knew it wouldn't be too long before we would be going into the next state, which would be Utah. But I was even more excited than that, because my wife had decided to drive to Ely, Nevada, where we would have a two-day rest. It would be the first time I had seen her in over a month. I looked forward to seeing her, and that put extra pep in my step. That day we walked our usual 35 miles. Going across Nevada we had to keep the mileage from 30 to 35 miles, due to the fact that it was such a long stretch to cross. We were on a time schedule and we were going to save our shorter days for when we would only be able to walk 12 to 18 miles. We wanted to get the bigger states out of the way. The more miles we got out of the way, the more grace time for the smaller states. So, everyone was really anxious to get through Nevada, after walking an average of 35 miles every day. We were all in good form by this time, being 90% of the way through Nevada, and we were all looking forward to that two-day rest in Ely, which was right down the road.

When we did get into Ely, thank goodness for good old plastic American Express. The first thing that was on my mind was to find me a cozy little motel and soak in the tub for a good hour and a half and totally relax. This I did. I stayed at the Full Moon Motel and booked a room for the two days that we would be there. I quickly got on the phone and called long distance back to Las Vegas and let Karen know the address of the motel I would be staying in.
After the call, I went back to the room, filled the tub, and soaked for at least a good hour before I went to bed. The next thing I knew there was a knock on the door. I peeked out the curtain, and I could see that it was Karen. I had fallen asleep for the whole time that she was making the drive from Las Vegas. It took her almost four hours. It was like a dream to me, because I had just talked to her and fell asleep, and it was like

she had just zapped herself there. I hadn't had to wait any time at all.

It was so great to see her. I gave her a big hug and a kiss and said, "Come on in to my little palace". We sat there and talked about the walk and the last month and a half, and reminisced. I caught up on the family gossip and had a relaxing two days in that town. We toured around the area, checking it out. We went out to eat, and had a great candlelit dinner. She had a nice outfit that I could change into. It was good to get out of my regular walking gear. I was pretty sick of looking at all the walking outfits I had been wearing for the last month. I figured, this is no fashion show, and who's going see me out here anyway? It was good to get into some of my regular clothes and go out to dinner with my wife. Seems like the two days went by in a snap, and next thing I knew she was dropping me off at the campsite, where the rest of the walkers were staying. She gave me a kiss and hug goodbye. She would be going back to Vegas, and I'd be back on that red road heading east.

Though I wanted to go back to Las Vegas with her, the spirits kept me strong and I continued on the Walk for Justice. As I watched her drive away from the campsite, I was very emotional and felt at odds with myself, but I knew in my heart that I couldn't go back yet. I had to continue to do what I knew had to be done. All of the other people on the Walk for Justice had become my second family, and I had become close to them, but I already missed Karen.

UTAH

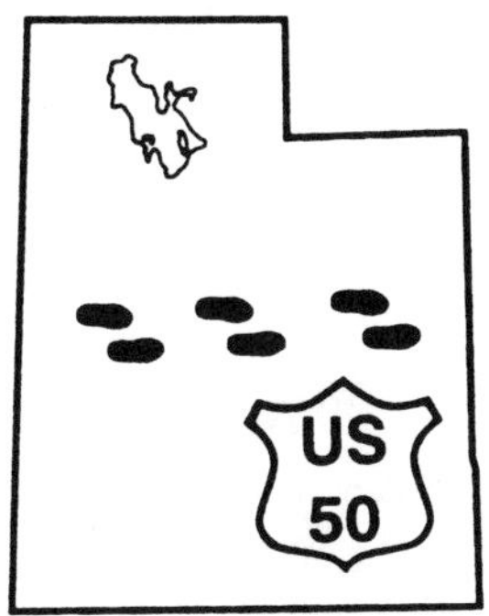

We crossed over the Nevada State line into Utah, and it was almost like a New Year's Eve party—without the alcohol. We all stood in Nevada and **jumped** over to Utah. Everybody said they didn't know if they wanted to stay in Nevada or go to Utah, and they kept jumping back and forth over the state line. I knew where I wanted to be - in Utah! We were only 10 states from D.C.: two states closer to reaching our goal. I was really glad to be off that long, lonely Nevada highway.

It was really a treat for me to be in Utah. I was from Wisconsin originally, but I had moved to Las Vegas with my wife. We had only been in Nevada for about four years. If you've ever been to Las Vegas, you know that there isn't as much greenery as there is back east. Seeing all that greenery in Utah, after nothing but desert for three weeks in Nevada, was a welcome sight. I really enjoyed the walk in Utah. I could smell the green vegetation and it was a true pleasure to be somewhere new.

We entered Utah, the land of the Ute and the Paiute on March 9. It would take us 342 miles to get across the state of Utah, but I wasn't worrying about that now. I was just happy to be in another state. I was leaving Nevada behind me and walking with nothing but good thoughts on my mind. I was thanking the Creator for letting myself and the rest of the walkers get this far without any major sicknesses or any serious injuries to any one of us.

We had made it about ten miles into Utah when we heard some beeping, and this van pulled up along side with three or four Indian brothers in it. They said to me, "We know this is the Walk for Justice. Where's Dennis Banks?" Dennis had gone into the nearest town to see if he could find shelter for the walkers in one of the churches or gyms, so I assumed responsibility and asked them what I could do for them. They told me they had been trying to catch up with us for a couple of days. They said they would just ride along, and when we got to the next camp they would take all of the walkers back into Nevada to a secret site where there were hot and cold springs. They wanted to honor the walkers by taking us to where we could relax our muscles and our sore feet. They said we could recharge our bodies so we could continue our walk in Utah.

It was a good thing to know that this open invitation was waiting for us at the end of the day, but I was not very anxious to get back into Nevada. It had taken us 450 miles and almost four weeks of walking to get through it. They explained, though, that we only had to go about twenty miles back into Nevada to this sacred water site, so I figured that this was as good a reason as any to go back in there. It didn't turn out to be such a bad thing after all.

We walked about fifteen miles into Utah and were taking our second half-hour break of the day, all spread out around this grassy area. We were eating a lunch that had been brought to us by a support vehicle. Dennis Banks pulled up when we were about fifteen minutes into our lunch break and said we would be covering about twenty-two miles that day, and a church would be putting us up for the night. A guy from the Shoshone Tribe had met with Dennis Banks. His name was Dennis Beeson, and he had explained to Dennis Banks about the sacred hot and cold springs that we were invited to. Dennis Banks told us we only had about another hour of walking, and then everyone who wanted to would get to go to these hot springs and relax. We were all looking forward to it.

After the half-hour break of talking to each other and taking in the sights we continued our walk across Utah.

We were walking down the road at a brisk pace, as we usually did, and I could see a vehicle coming up over the horizon. As it got closer we found out it was a news reporter from the Utah Daily Herald. He pulled up and said that we must be the people from the Walk for Justice. He said they heard about the Walk and wanted to talk to someone about the march we had been on for a month or so. I told him who I was and that I was one of the two main Staff carriers. I explained that I would be more than happy to talk with him at the end of the day's walk. We only had a half-hour longer to walk and we would be finished for the day, so we set up an interview. We were all happy that the news media was picking up on our walk, getting the information out to the people in Utah about what we were doing. I had a real good interview with this gentleman. The paper was one of the big newspapers in Utah, so we were all pretty happy that they cared enough to do an article on us. The next day, sure enough, we were on the front page in The Utah Daily Herald Newspaper. It was good to know that the people in Utah were interested. In fact, as it turned out, the people in Utah were instrumental in helping us with the walk and with Leonard Peltier's case. We are really grateful to the people in Utah who helped us out. They treated us with a lot of respect and kindness.

It had gotten back to Dennis Banks that I was the person who the newspaper had interviewed, so he came to me and told me he would like to make me the official spokesperson for the Walk for Justice. "Anytime any news people come upon the walk and want to speak to somebody about it, I would appreciate it if you took on the responsibility, since you are one of the Staff carriers and you have a good way with words." I gladly accepted, because I did find it fairly easy to talk to the media. Being somewhat of ham, I wasn't nervous, and I felt like I handled my first interview pretty well. So I decided to take on the responsibility, and that was one of my official duties from that point on until the end of the walk.

That night, after setting up camp, having supper and saying prayers at the circle, Dennis Banks organized the support vehicles to take anyone who wanted to go, back to the sacred springs. Everyone got their towels and swimming suits and took the 20-mile ride back into Nevada. When we saw the sign saying "Welcome to Nevada", it was like thanks, but no thanks.

It was dark by the time we got to the sacred springs. Everyone took turns going from the hot to the cold. We stayed there about two hours and it was well received. Talk about recharging. I felt like I had a total body massage from a professional masseuse. It was 100% satisfying. We all gathered in a circle to recite sacred prayers thanking Mother Earth for giving us the hot springs. We loaded back into the vans and started the journey back to Utah.

When we arrived at the campsite we had another prayer ceremony, a feast, and a drum ceremony. We spent time afterwards, talking with the Shoshone brothers that we had met. We shook hands and thanked them for inviting us to the sacred springs. After they left, we all went to sleep, rejuvenated from the springs, but tired from the walk, knowing what would greet us the next day.

But the next morning, the wake-up call from Rooster would be a little different. One of the walkers took it upon himself to play a prank on old Rooster by taking his bullhorn. Rooster was somewhat upset about it, and at the morning circle Dennis Banks asked for the person responsible for taking Rooster's bullhorn to please return it. Sometime during the day, it resurfaced suspiciously in one of the support vehicles. At the break in the afternoon, Rooster told Dennis that somebody had returned his bullhorn and he was quite pleased. That wasn't the last time that would happen. Rooster's bullhorn came up missing on several occasions, but it always seemed to turn back up. We never knew who the prankster was. Everybody thought it was funny to see Rooster in search of his bullhorn. Old Rooster just wasn't the same without that bullhorn to wake people up. Somehow, it did manage to stay with the group for the entire journey to D.C.

As I said, Utah was one of the most pleasant states, even though we had to walk 325 miles. The people made our passing through very pleasant, and we had a lot of news coverage. The Salt Lake Tribune also covered the walk, and we were thankful for that. The third newspaper that gave us coverage was the Desert News of Utah County. All in all, three major newspapers had covered the Walk for Justice, bringing more attention to the Leonard Peltier case.

On the fourteenth day of walking through Utah we met back up with the medicine man, Bear Boy, who had said sacred prayers for us back in Nevada. He caught up with us to say more sacred prayers and make sure that everybody was being kept spiritually well. He also helped to set up a sweat with the Ute people on the last day in Utah. It was a very moving and spiritual sweat ceremony, with Bear Boy saying all the prayers. It was one of the finest sweats I had ever been involved with. It gave me the strength to carry on through this journey.

It was evident that the Creator was watching over us. We really didn't have any extremely bad weather to complain about, other than a couple of snowy days up in the Sierras. Up to this time, the walk was pretty comfortable weather wise, and this kept everyone in good spirits. Walking is one thing, but if it can be a good walk versus a bad, snowy walk, I'm all for the good walk.

It was almost like the state of Utah treated the Walk for Justice too well. Everybody was really sorry to be leaving, but we were also very excited about getting into our fourth state, which was Colorado. Morale was high. We knew it wouldn't be long until we got to the Colorado line.

I was really excited because I had always heard about how beautiful Colorado was. I wanted to see for myself what was true and what wasn't. I had heard about the infamous Monarch Pass that was 11,312 feet high. I was overly anxious to see this for myself.

We came across some people who had just left Colorado. They said that it was pretty cold there, and it had been snowing a lot. That wasn't what I had wanted to hear, because you know I'm not very fond of the cold; but snow on top of cold? I figured I had better psyche myself up for this, and be ready for the worst. If it wasn't as bad as I expected, then I would get through it a lot easier.

With that on my mind, I crawled into my tent and prepared myself for the walk into Colorado, sometime the next day - February 25th. I quickly fell asleep.

In the morning we didn't get our usual rude awakening by the almighty Rooster, and everybody slept in real hard until about 9:00 AM. The first thing I heard that day was somebody screaming "Where do you think you are, keeping these hotel/motel hours here? Everybody get up!" We then found out at the morning circle that Rooster, himself, had overslept and gave us a few extra hours of sleep. We were all happy about that, since he usually woke us up at 5:00 in the morning. We were usually already on the road by 7:30 or 8:00.

You could say the few extra hours of sleep we had were good for some and bad for others, for the simple reason that we had to make up for lost time. At the morning circle, Dennis Banks brought everyone up-to-date on the latest issues and said that he wanted to make sure the people were listening to the Staff carriers, Dale VanFleet and myself, because the Highway Patrol had complained about the Walk for Justice being too far out in the road. They had told Dennis in a nice way and he was telling us in a nice way, too. He was stressing about how to keep to the right of the line and stay real nice and tight so we didn't have to hear any more complaints. He also explained that the Staff carriers and himself were not leaders. He said the leaders on the walk were the Eagle Staffs we were carrying. Those eagle feathers were the leaders, and all the walkers were to respect that Eagle Staff and in return respect the Staff carriers.

At times, we all had our little squabbles and Dennis would try to iron everything out during the morning circle. If anyone had any gripes or disagreements they would be taken care of before starting the day's walk. If anything got out of hand, it always got straightened out at morning circle.

After the morning circle and the latest gossip, we had a drum ceremony and a prayer to the Creator and we saged off. Everyone then fell into a formation and headed out for the last 30 miles of this state. We were happy and excited about this last leg of our journey in Utah.

We walked real hard on this last day. It was a very special day for myself. I'm very fond of the Bald Eagle, which is very sacred to the American Indian. Midway through the day, we happened to look up and see a bald eagle circling over us. He stayed with us for about half an hour. It was a real good sign for me-real sacred. It made my day very special because, being a city boy from good old Milwaukee, it was the first bald eagle I had ever seen in flight. It was a phenomenal thing to see. It just put more pep in my step, and kept me going strong. It was a reassuring sign from the Creator, as far as I was concerned.

We had a good, hard walk that day, even after taking a lunch break and several "smoke" breaks for the smokers. Dennis Banks had come to the decision that we had to meet their needs just like everyone else's. But, since this was a spiritual walk, he didn't want anyone smoking in formation with the Staff, so we decided to take breaks every five miles for the people that smoked. It worked out real well.

About five miles from the Colorado border, people that had brought food or donated money and had come out to hear Dennis Banks speak about the cause and why we were walking, met up with us and walked with us to the state line. I was very moved because there were women and children, and the mothers were pushing their kids in strollers. All in all there were about 15 walkers that donated part of the day and walked with us the rest of the way out of Utah. It was real moving to see people of all ages participate and do their part in the walk. We were really surprised that they still hadn't gotten enough of the Walk for Justice. Even after all they had done for us in Utah, they still had to come out and walk the last five miles with us. At the end of that five miles we lined up in a circle and said prayers, had a drum ceremony and saged off. We thanked those people for taking the time to walk with us. After the ceremony the people who had walked with us said their good-byes. We were sorry to see them leave because we had made good friends with some of these people.

It was a strange feeling, because we never knew if we would ever see any of these friends again.

COLORADO

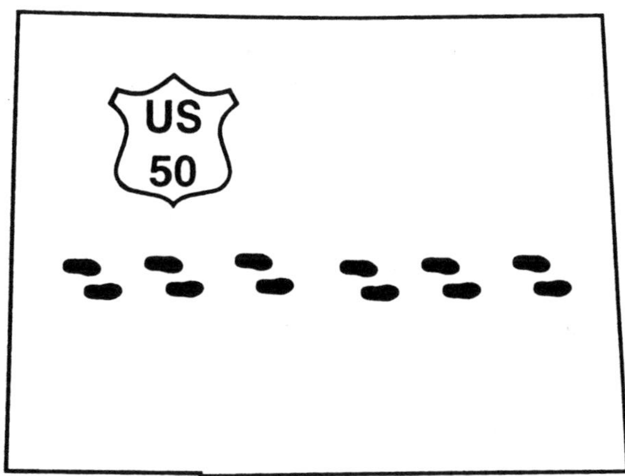

Getting a late start like we did on that particular day we crossed into Colorado just about dark. Another state down, and everybody was having something like a little party in their minds, just expressing their feelings and saying how glad they were that we were getting closer. There were a lot of high fives and hugs, and all kinds of funny things going on, as far as what people were celebrating about. We were just plain happy to finish out another state without any major mishaps or anything. We knew the Great Spirit was watching over us, and we had that Eagle Staff.

I felt real good knowing that I was in for a new change of scenery, and whatever lay ahead was welcome. We walked into the town of Grand Junction, Colorado on the 25th of March. It would take us 25 days to get up and over the mountains, then across the rest of the state, a distance of 471 miles.

The people of Grand Junction, Colorado were waiting for us. They had heard about the Walk for Justice coming across the state from the news media. They were excited to meet with the people of the walk and find out what the walk was all about, one on one, and wanted to contribute what they could, as far as food and shelter. Our first day in Colorado was a good one. They put us up in a church and had a real nice welcoming dinner for us. In turn, we honored them with our native spiritual drum songs and thanked them. We became friends with a lot of people in the town of Grand Junction right off the bat.

In the small amount of time that we had been in Colorado we had gotten over 1500 signatures on Leonard Peltier's Walk for Justice clemency petition. People were coming out in droves to learn more and find out what they could do to help his case. We had to set up a spokesperson to do seminars to inform people about the Peltier case and make people more aware of ways to support the Walk for Justice and the causes. We were pretty excited at this point.

A man named Don who had heard Dennis Banks speak, welcomed the people from the walk, and invited us to his house. He had a large teepee set up in his back yard, and he had a Sweat Lodge. He invited people from the walk to come over and sweat. He ran this all day and all night long so everyone could recharge themselves and have a place to pray in the Sweat Lodge. People who didn't know about the

Sweat Lodge, who lived in Grand Junction, were invited to come. He wanted them to be aware of what the sacred Sweat Lodge was all about. We had two days off, and a lot of the walkers spent their time there. He made us feel right at home.   He brought to Dennis Banks' and my attention, that in Gunnison there was a white buffalo on a game farm. He asked us if the people would want to shuttle out and see it. Of course, with the buffalo being sacred to the American Indian, especially a white buffalo, we wasted no time in saying "Let's get out there". They set up a shuttle in Gunnison with support vehicles, back and forth all day to view this white buffalo. This was important enough for me to bring out my camera, and when it came time for me to go out to this reserve, which was about 15 minutes away from the Sweat Lodge, I was very excited. On the way, we saw two golden eagles sitting in a tree. I told the guy driving the van, "Hey, you gotta stop. There's two golden eagles sitting in that tree". I told him that I had to have their picture. I was so excited. We stopped at the side of the road and I jumped out of the van in such a hurry that I fell into a ditch about four feet deep. I had to laugh, laying there in the ditch, camera in hand. I was glad that I was the one with the camera. After climbing my way out of the ditch, I got my pictures of the two golden eagles and got back into the van.

About five minutes later we were there. We pulled in and it was easy to see the white buffalo off in the distance in a gated open field. We got out of the van and went up to the railing. He was about 30 feet away. We were observing the white buffalo, and he was observing us. There was a safety fence and another fence behind the safety fence, but for some reason I felt I had to get closer, so I climbed over the first fence and got in between the two fences. I **really** wanted a close up shot of this sacred white buffalo. I noticed all this white hair stuck on the barbwire fence as I was walking along. It was from the buffalo scratching his body up against the barbwire. I started collecting the hair off the wire until I had about a silver dollar sized hand full. I put it in my Medicine Pouch. What more could I want. I took several pictures of this white buffalo and got some of his hair. It made me feel real good. We stayed out here around 20 minutes, and with white buffalo treasures, plus the pictures of the golden eagles, it turned out to be a very special 25 minutes. I thanked the Creator for letting us see the golden eagles and the white buffalo. I thanked him for letting me get some of this sacred hair.

After saying the prayer to the white buffalo I made a tobacco tie and tied it to the fence post in white buffalo's honor. We got in the van and went back, so other people could get out and see this sacred animal.

We went got back to Don's house where we were having the sweats, and the people from Grand Junction were preparing a feast. We were going to have a pow wow and a ceremony to thank these people, and everyone was pretty excited. I was extra hungry at this point in time. It was a welcome sight to see all this food. What especially caught my eye was this bucket of Kentucky Fried Chicken. I knew I was going to be in line to get a piece of that bird.

The feast was ready around 6:00 that night. We all gathered in a sacred circle and saged off. The people from Grand Junction thanked us for sharing our knowledge with them, and we thanked **them** for everything they had done for us since we had gotten there. Dennis Banks said that for the two days we were off, we could stay at the church, or we could stay at Don's house. Some people would stay in his teepee and others would camp out around the teepee. I decided to sleep at the church.

Dennis also mentioned the fact that we would be going to Sand Creek to visit that site. It was a sacred site to us because a lot of Indian people were killed out there in the Sand Creek massacre. We would be going there to pray for our people and to honor all the people that had died there. We were all looking forward to this ceremony. In addition, Dennis also mentioned that we would be going to the Colorado State Penitentiary in Florence. The men who wanted to go would have to sign up on a list. They would only be taking 10 to 15 people at the most, so the first to sign up would be the first to go. This interested me, because I knew something about what the Indian brothers were going through. I wanted to meet and talk with them and be a part of that. I was going to sign up, but with the feast and all the goings on, I forgot to put my name on the list.

I was disappointed about that, but a couple of days later Dennis and I talked and he said that he would see what he could do to get me in. Bear Boy, the Ute medicine man had shown up at our campsite on the second day, and he was the one that organized this approved list of 15 of the Indian walkers, including Dennis Banks and myself, to get into this prison and sweat with our Indian brothers. He had his connections because he worked with the prisons in Colorado. He would be one of the main speakers in the sweat because he was a medicine man, and the prayers he offered would be really strong. They sent in the list of 15 people, and since I had forgotten to sign up, I wasn't on the list. One of the people that wanted to go had changed his mind at the last minute, so Dennis came to me and said "Hey, Kindness. If you want to go on this sweat in the penitentiary, we're going to have to work out a plan. This list of 15 walkers has been pre-approved, so if they don't ask for identification you have to go in there as the guy who was supposed to go. His name is Dave Moran, so just remember that your name is not Kindness for that day".

That's what we did on our day off, but soon it was time to get reacquainted with good old 50. Up to this time, we had had all good weather on this Colorado Highway. No snow, it was windy and cold, but at least it was not freezing. Any colder, and it would have been uncomfortable for me. We all managed, even though it was quite windy at times. People that were coming through the part of Colorado that we were walking through said that it was getting colder, the closer you got to the mountains, and it had been snowing. It was only natural. We were preparing ourselves for the worst, hoping we would get through Colorado without any major snowstorms or blizzards. We continued to walk, hoping that everything would continue going as well as it had, up to this point.

One day we were about 15 miles into our designated walk, when two school buses went by and then stopped. Two guys got out and said, "You're on the Walk for Justice?" He said, "We have school kids here, and we heard about your walk across the country that you're doing for Leonard Peltier. We saw it on the news." He told us that they were on a field trip today and they had decided to hunt us down. It was their understanding that we were on Highway 50, and they had driven for about an hour and a half to find us. They wanted to know if it would be OK to walk with us most of the day. It was fine by Dennis Banks and me. The only thing was, they had to make sure they had their own water and comfortable shoes, and they were to stay to the right of the white line. Most of the time there was three feet of space across the line. Everyone had to stay in single file so we wouldn't have any accidents. Everybody introduced themselves, and we formed a circle and saged everybody off. They knew why we were walking because they had been following the case. With that, we got back into formation and continued our walk. There were approximately 60 high school students walking with us for the day. We were all pretty happy to see some new faces, and Dennis Banks told me to slow the pace down. We were all pretty good walkers by now, and could keep up quite a brisk pace. Many times, people would say "Tell Kindness to slow down." I would have to slow down so people could keep up, because I had my mind on the goal and would sometimes forget that there were people behind me. It was almost like I was in a trance. So, Dennis reminded me to walk a little easy, and I did.

With the high school walkers we had to take a few more breaks than we normally would, but these kids were donating their energy and their feet for a cause that we all supported. During the breaks we got acquainted with all the students. They were curious to know what I was carrying and what the feathers were about. I explained who I was, why I was on the Walk, and that I was one of the two main Staff carriers, why there were eagle feathers on the Staff. I told them how everybody followed the Staff because it was our leader. We all followed the Staff as one. Also, I explained how the red, yellow, white, and black ribbons signified the four races. I told them that we were not only walking across the country for Leonard Peltier, but for all races to come together and stop the raping of Mother Earth; to have people take a closer look at all the devastation being done. I told them to appreciate the fact that Mother Earth was here for us to walk upon, and how we should treat her like we would our own mother. I also explained that through all the miles and almost two months that we had been walking, out of all the streams and little ponds and lakes that I had seen, not one was fit to drink out of.

There was always a sign that read, "Not fit for human consumption." Although these lakes and ponds looked like the pictures you see on the back a nature calendar, you couldn't drink out of them. It just showed how big companies, and individual people alike, had been treating Mother Earth, when the water from the streams and lakes that were out in the middle of nowhere wasn't fit to drink.

The day went well with these kids. They learned a lot and were real interested. They all signed our Leonard Peltier Petition for executive clemency, and they also left a money donation of over $150.00. They said they would be coming to our next campsite to bring food. Dennis thanked them, and told them that we had been invited to a sweat, and to honor them for their help, he had asked the person who invited us if it would be OK if they sweated too. The students didn't know what a sweat was, but they said that they would come out. We told them they were welcome to come and sweat with real Indians. At that point, everybody started laughing.

That evening around seven o'clock, we went to where we were going to have the sweat. It was on the property of a friend of Dennis Banks, and surprisingly, most of the students did show up. A lot of them were amazed at how hot it was in the Sweat Lodge. Dennis had told them that if anyone had health problems like high or low blood pressure, then they would be entering the Sweat Lodge at their own risk. Not everyone could stay all four rounds. Some people asked to go out because it had gotten too hot, but that was to be expected for someone who had never been in a sweat. They do get very hot. All in all, most of the students went into the sweat, and really enjoyed what they learned throughout the day with us. They enjoyed walking with us, praying with us, participating in sacred drum songs, and saging off. About ten o'clock everything ended and we all said our good-byes. Everyone said they would be praying for us and watching the news for information as to how the walk was going.

One of the teachers had some kind of pull over at the College and worked it out so we could stay in their gymnasium for a week. We would be shuttling to our designated mile marker and it would be marked where we stopped. Then, buses would come to pick us up and shuttle us back to the University where we would sleep for the night. They would then shuttle us out in the morning, back to the point where we had stopped, and we would continue walking. This was really convenient, because every day that week we knew we would be shuttled back to the University to spend the night. We wouldn't have to set up any tents or look for a place to stay. We had a whole week of being assured of having shelter, food, and warmth. The farther along we got, the longer it took us to get back to the University, but once we got on the buses we kicked off our shoes and people fell asleep, or did what they wanted to do. It was a relaxing ride back to the University.

The university took very good care of us. We set up a seminar, getting signatures, selling T-shirts and Peltier pins, and Dennis Banks' new tape called "Still Strong." We not only had shelter and comfort, but we were also making money by selling our Peltier items. We were actually making more money than we had expected. We were getting donations and making more people aware of what was going on. The people on campus were finding out about us, and what we stood for.

In addition, they let us have the movie theater to show the movie "Incident at Oglala". That was the movie that Robert Redford had made about the Leonard Peltier story. That helped to teach them why we were walking. They showed the movie every night at eight o'clock, and surprisingly it was a packed house every time it was shown.

Also, the cafeteria fed us free of charge the whole week we were there - breakfast and dinner. We weren't there for lunch, but we looked forward to that good cafeteria (close to being home cooked) food. They also had a Taco Bell, and everybody from the Walk got a stamp that let us go in there any time, day or night, and have free food and beverages. The University also picked up this tab. It was phenomenal how well they took care of us for that whole week. It was almost like I was in College, going back there every night. I was really getting used to the place, and I was sorry to leave. But, just like so many other towns and places we had come through, it was time to leave and move on down the road. We had a job to do. We had to keep walking.

A lot of the core walkers that had been most of the way from Sacramento until now, and other walkers that had joined in on the way, seemed to be getting tired and exhausted, even though we were taking breaks. Dennis came to me and suggested that I get up at three or four in the morning and get started on the Walk. There would be a support vehicle behind me, so I would walk as many miles as I could, at my own pace. Then, when the rest of the walkers got up they would be shuttled to wherever they would find me, regardless of whether I had covered 10 miles, 20 miles or whatever. For instance, on a 28 mile day I had got up at 4:00 o'clock in the morning and covered 12 or 13 miles in four hours time. Then the bulk of the walkers would catch up to me and we would finish the rest of the miles together. That would be fewer miles for the bulk of the walkers and more for me. I considered myself to be a very strong individual, and people were looking to me for that leadership. I thanked the Creator for making me strong and keeping me strong. I had no problem with it and told Dennis I would be willing to do that.

Dale VanFleet, the other staff carrier, and myself were covering a lot of miles together. Everybody was getting more rest and this continued like a relay throughout the rest of the walk. Sometimes I didn't want to be around a lot of other people anyway. Sometimes I would get up at two o'clock in the morning and make it a point to see how fast I could go and how many miles I could walk. There were times when I would get to the designated spot where we were to stop for the day before the rest of the walkers even caught up, and they wouldn't even have to walk at all that day. Some people were happy about that and some weren't. They would be saying "Damn, Kindness, save us some miles. We want to walk, too."

Sometimes it was a no win situation, but it never got out of hand. We did what we had to do. Together, sometimes with the bulk of the walkers and sometimes without, we got the job done, just like the Creator and Dennis Banks had asked us to do.

One time, I went to Dennis and asked him to have Dave Patton, the main guy who followed behind in a pick-up truck, get me up at 1:00 in the morning. It would be Dave's job to set the alarm and get me up. The only people on the road that day would be Dave Patton, his wife Linda, their 10-year-old son, and me. The four of us would get ready and take off to the spot where we had stopped the day before, and try to get in as many miles as we could before the bulk of the walkers showed up. They carried water, fruit, and a lot of carbohydrates, and they took care of me. They watched my back and made sure that there were no crazy people driving stupid that would hit me. They had an orange day glow banner on the back of their pick-up that said " Caution - Walkers Ahead".

We were midway through the Colorado Rocky Mountains, and we came upon a place where there was a lot of construction going on. They said that this road was going to be closed after 8:00 AM because they were going to be blasting. We were 10 miles out from the campsite and we decided that Dave would have to ride back and tell them that they weren't going to be able to get through the mountain range area until after 4:00 PM. That meant I wouldn't have Dave to watch my back, since there could be no vehicles on the road until after four. He gave me enough water to fill my canteen, then he and his family turned around to inform Dennis and the rest of the walkers that they should just sit tight and relax until 4:00 PM, which would be the whole day. They had a whole extra day in camp to rest before catching up with me later that day. I continued walking.

This was a very enjoyable day for me because I had the whole road to myself. I felt like the "King of the Road". I had nobody to bother me, nobody asking me for a smoke break, nobody asking me to slow up, and I didn't have to worry about vehicles behind me because the road was closed. It was a very beautiful Rocky Mountain area, with the Tomichi River winding alongside the road. Knowing I could walk at my own pace because people weren't going to be catching up to me till four was really enjoyable. I wanted to cover as many miles as I possibly could. Perhaps, get the whole mileage done so all we would have to do is make camp when they caught up with me. I walked all day and saw a lot of wildlife, including mountain goats, a Bald Eagle, and a couple of coyotes. I had my army fatigue pants full of fruit and carbohydrates, and I had plenty of water. It was one of my more enjoyable and memorable days. I even got to a telephone and called my wife. I didn't have to worry about anybody saying "I'm next in line. Could you hurry up." It was just a great day, one of my favorite days on the whole trip.

The bulk of the walkers caught up to me when I had covered 24 miles. I had no problem with that because it left me and the rest of the walkers about six more miles to go. When we got to our campsite we had the circle, and Dennis thanked me for walking. We all saged off, put our tents up, and relaxed. We had our usual gossip session and drum ceremonies. I retired to my tent and wrote a letter to my wife. I was looking forward to getting it in the mail the next day. That summed up that day and that night. It was a good one.

We were getting higher and higher into the mountains, very close to Monarch Pass. We were getting into the cold and into the snow. The next day, the Highway Patrol stopped and told us that for own safety they suggested we didn't walk through this particular area this day because there were avalanches. Dennis Banks told the State Trooper that we had a schedule to keep, and we needed to get through this area. The trooper said he couldn't tell us that we **couldn't** walk through the area but he **could** say that we **shouldn't**. But, if we decided to do it, we would have to go through the mountain range area where there had been avalanches. We all said, hey, we've come this far and we're being watched over. We have the eagle feather Staff and everything to see us through, so we continued through the avalanche area.

We made it through there safely, and we completed the day's walk.

Later, we found out that in one of the areas we had gone through there had been an avalanche about forty five minutes after we passed. I can truthfully say that the spirits were watching over all of us. That road had to be closed down for a day and a half to clear the snow. That would have set us back two days. We thanked the Great Spirit for watching over us and getting us through there safely and without any delays.

The next morning, in the circle, Dennis made it clear that we would be crossing Monarch Pass that day, at an elevation of 11,312 feet. It would be a 42-mile day. Anybody that didn't think they could make it would have to ride. Dale, 60% of the walkers and myself, said we wanted to walk over Monarch Pass. We all saged off and had our prayer ceremony, thanking the Creator for getting us this far safe and sound. Dave Patton and his wife and son were at the back of us as we started the climb up Monarch Pass. It was very sunny and we saw a couple of Bald Eagles, which let us know the day was going to be good. We thanked the Creator for sending the Eagles our way and started to walk.

We got about eight miles into the walk and it started snowing. At first it was light, but then it continued to pick up and it got worse as the minutes and miles went on. Dennis had already gone up and over Monarch Pass to the church where we would be staying, along with some of the other people that didn't want to walk over the pass. They went on to the next campsite to set it up for the people walking this 42-mile trek. The Park Rangers came rolling up to tell us they were going to be closing the Monarch Pass area due to severe weather and blizzard conditions. That meant we were going to have to get in vehicles and get over, or stay on the other side until it clears because they had a road block gate which automatically closed the road. With this in mind, Dave Patton loaded people in the truck.

Another support vehicle had come back and they were shuttling people over Monarch pass. For some odd reason, I told Dave Patton to shuttle everyone across and I would cover the whole distance by myself. I didn't want to come back the next day and be a day behind. It would be safer to get these vehicles off the pass due to icy conditions and I'd just go ahead and walk over. I would be totally safe on foot.

At this point, somewhat of an argument transpired, with people saying there would be no one here to watch me. I told them I was a grown man, I was carrying the Staff, and I would assume the responsibility and the danger. I asked to be left alone so I could complete the Monarch Pass. Dave and his wife didn't think it was a good idea. I finally convinced them that I was a big boy and I was going to do it, with them there or without them. With the road getting icier by the minute I told them to get on the other side of the pass and I would handle it. Dave made sure I had plenty of water. I had some dried strawberries and dried buffalo that some people had donated. Dave told me he couldn't say he didn't warn me and I told him not to worry about it. I watched the truck disappear into the whirlwind of snow and I actually felt good about being left alone at that particular time. I told myself I could handle it, because there was only one way up the road and one way down. It was just the Eagle Staff in my hand and me.

I decided to put extra pep in my step to get over this mountain as quickly as my body would allow me to. Even if the others thought I was crazy, I knew the Creator was on my side. My faith and belief in Leonard's cause was the fuel I needed to keep going.

I had never been at this altitude before and found out it wasn't going to be as easy as I had thought. Each breath got harder and harder. The higher I got, the harder it was to breathe. In fact, I was getting flu-like symptoms. I later found out that I was experiencing altitude sickness. All the while I was walking, the snow was very thick. The flakes were almost like fairy tale snowflakes. I was really enjoying myself with all the peace and quiet I was having. It reminded me of playing in the snow when I was a kid. I felt like I was the king of the mountain again, up there all by myself, with no vehicles on a closed road. It was up to me to get up and over on my own. I knew it wasn't a do or die situation, but I knew it could be if I let it. I just continued walking strong, thinking about various situations in my life, and reviewing the walk in my mind. How nice it was to be on Monarch pass all by myself.

It seemed like I had been walking about two hours and the snow had not let up, but I really wasn't worried. There were no vehicles up there to clear the roads, and the snow was falling pretty fast. So, the higher I got, the deeper the snow was getting. That slowed me down. I was starting to get snow in my boots, and my main concern, even though my boots were water proofed and very good boots, was to keep the snow out so I wouldn't get frostbite. The effort to keep snow out of my boots slowed me down. I had no gloves, and all I had was a sock-cap to cover my head. I had taken my jacket off earlier, because I was getting too hot during the conversation when Dave Patton told me it wasn't a good idea to walk, and I said I was walking. You really couldn't call it an argument. But, I had put my jacket in the back of the cab and they were long gone. I had forgotten I didn't have a jacket on. As a matter of fact, it was about an hour before I noticed I didn't have my jacket on. I was wearing a rather thick sweatshirt and the snow was wet. It landed on me and froze, acting like a layer of insulation.

Walking nonstop at the pace I was keeping also helped to keep me relatively warm. I had pulled my hands up into my sweatshirt and knotted my sleeves off, so my body heat was conserved. I wasn't freezing, but I knew that at night the weather would change drastically and the temperature would drop, so my main concern was to walk as fast as I could before night got here. Saying heavy prayers to the Creator and talking to that Eagle Staff, I continued to walk strong, and I walked the rest of the day. I sang some Indian songs to myself and thought about meeting my wife in Colorado Springs, which was on the other side of Monarch Pass. This kept me going.

I got midway through Monarch Pass and the snow started to slow down. It was a slow snowfall, and I really wasn't worried because I had made it through the worst part. But, I had to walk through the deep snow that had accumulated. I really didn't want to rest because I didn't want to cool down, so it was a constant trot and a walk and a half run that I did down the backside of the mountain. It was relatively easy because I was on my descent. I slipped a couple of times and laughed to myself - if someone would see me now. I had slipped on several occasions, but never let the Eagle Staff fall out of my hand and hit the ground.

Those who know about eagle feathers know that you do not want them to hit the ground. Anytime you're at a pow wow and drop an Eagle Feather off your Indian regalia the medicine person at the pow wow will sage off the feather before it's picked up off the ground, out of respect. I didn't have to worry about that because I didn't let the Eagle Staff hit the ground. The last time I fell down, I noticed that the eagle feathers were frozen in place. I told myself that I had better step the hardest I had ever stepped up to this time. I was joking with myself about anything and everything. I wasn't worried, because I knew I had the situation under control. But there were times when I had my doubts, because I didn't know how long this road was or how far I had covered. I usually had a back-up vehicle telling me how many miles we had covered. I felt I was about 80% on the down side of Monarch Pass.

A snowplow approached, which meant to me that they were getting ready to open the gate to allow people over Monarch Pass. While I was coming down, people were going up. No vehicles were coming behind me, so the area I had just come through was still closed. The driver of a camper that was coming up the hill was rather amazed to see me. He asked me where I was coming from and I explained that I was one of the people from the Walk for Justice. They had heard about the walk because they were from the town next to Gunnison. But, you had to go up and over Monarch Pass to get to Gunnison. He said he saw a bunch of people ride into town in a van that said Walk for Justice and he was wondering why **they** were in town and **I** was here. I briefly explained to him that I took it upon myself to walk the Pass so everyone else could get into town. It was safer for one person to walk versus a bunch of people. He asked me how it looked down on the other side, and I told him it was snowing pretty hard. He said they were going to open it up on the other end or they wouldn't have let his camper through.

Shortly after that, I did hear a vehicle coming up behind me. I could see that he had snow chains on, and I knew that Monarch Pass was reopened. One person pulled along side and asked if I needed a ride, and I said "No, thank you". I told them I had to complete the rest of the miles, and at no time was I supposed to stop walking and accept a ride. I had never ridden any length of the way from San Francisco to this present point and I wasn't about to do it now.

I got to the bottom of Monarch Pass and I saw the Walk for Justice van. Dennis and A.J., another walker, and the driver were in it, and A.J. told me they were starting to get worried about me. They said they wanted to take a picture of me. Little did I know I had snow piled up on my stocking cap. I looked kind of like the abominable snowman, all covered in snow and the Eagle Staff with its feathers frozen in place. Dennis asked if I wanted some hot coffee. I told him I wasn't a coffee drinker, but thanks anyway. He told me it was about 13 miles to the town where we were camped at a church. He wanted to know if I wanted to hop in and get a ride, and we could start from that point in the morning. I said no, I wanted to complete the rest of the walk into town. He said I just needed to stay on Highway 50 and when I got to town they would have a vehicle waiting to direct me. He said that once I got off that road, I would have to go through a part of the city and they didn't want me to get lost.

Dennis said "You're a good man and we love you." They left me there and I continued until I finished the 13 miles, which was all flat and icy. But, there was no snow. I was glad I had covered the whole distance up and over Monarch Pass. I felt very strong about that. It was great to know I only had 13 miles to go. I continued to walk and an occasional car whizzed by me. I was the only person out there walking down that snow-covered road. I was getting some pretty strange looks. I had to walk through this ski area where all the skiers hung out. There were various bars and gas stations and I had to walk through this populated area. People were looking at me like "What is this all about? Who are you, or matter of fact **what** are you?" No real bad negative looks, just surprised stares. Certain people would stop and ask what I was doing. I would quickly explain to them and they would say, "Hey, good luck" and leave it at that.

I had started the walk over Monarch Pass at 8:00 in the morning, in a group with the rest of the people, and I had covered a total of 42 miles - most of it in a blizzard. I felt good about it and was proud of myself. I finally reached the vehicle that was coming out to see how close I was to the spot that Dennis Banks had told me about. They came up to me with hot apple cider and a sandwich, and told me I was about six miles from the church. They asked me if I wanted a ride. I told them no, I came this far and I'll finish it. They gave me directions so I could walk through the town.

It was good to walk through a town. I started seeing stuff that brought back good memories, like Pizza Hut and McDonald's. I had to walk about five miles through this town to get to the church. I was walking down a city street with a rough idea of where the church would be, because I had stopped and asked somebody. They told me to go down two blocks and turn to the right. I could see the steeple about a block away and knew that had to be it. In addition, I could hear the welcome sound of drumming. Little did I know that somebody had come out and saw me with the staff, and they were welcoming me with a drum ceremony. Everybody gave me hugs, handshakes, and high fives. They had a drum ceremony honoring me and saged me off.

After that I changed into dry clothing. I had a nice hot meal and was glad to be back with my second family. After the meal, people asked me how it felt to be king of the mountain, up there on my own. I told them I had loved every minute of it. Dennis came over and said that they were really proud of me. He shook my hand and found me a nice spot under one of the tables in the church. I put my sleeping bag under it, and I think I went into a coma.

After crossing Monarch Pass we had four days of rest. It was during this time that Dennis Banks, fourteen other people and myself signed up to visit the Indian inmates. We prepared ourselves for this visit and would be taking a van over to Florence, Colorado.

We pulled up to the prison and saw this real intimidating looking structure behind the two, double barbwire fences. There were six different prison facilities in this area and we were at the main one, which was maximum security. We walked up to the reception desk and Dennis handed him the list of people that would be going in. The guard said, "As I call your name off, step over to the metal detector."

We all lined up and he called our names off, one-by-one. When he called Dave Moran, I stepped through the metal detector and I was in like Flynn, as the old saying goes. I found it somewhat humorous. Usually you want to break out, but on this particular day, **I** would be sneaking **into** a prison. It was kind of a good feeling deep down inside. I was just happy that I was able to get in.

Once we were all approved and got in, the guard told us to stay in a single line. That wasn't hard at all. We were all used to doing that, walking single file down those long roads. No problem! He took us through different areas of the prison compound where various inmates were saying "Hi" and waving to us. He took us to this corner of the prison yard where the Indian brothers were waiting. They had their Sweat Lodge set up and they were ready to go.

They gave us strong handshakes and a very warm welcome. They were very glad to meet Dennis Banks and the rest of us. Many of these Indian brothers were past and present AIM members, and they were really anxious to meet some people that were doing something for the cause. With Leonard Peltier being in prison himself, they were glad to see that we had been approved and had gotten in.

We were ready to have our sweat ceremony. They had lunch for us, and we ate the same food that the prisoners ate. They brought us out box lunches and we chatted back and forth and got to know each other. The prisoners were real interested in the walk, and who had walked the farthest, and what was the most exciting part of the trip so far. They heard about us in the newspapers and on the radio. In some of the areas of the prison where they had TV, they had seen us. They felt that they were a part of the Walk by being able to talk to us, knowing that at the end of the day, we would be going back to freedom. It was just a real big treat for them, and for us, it was kind of sad. We felt bad for them, but Creator knew what He was doing. One particular Indian brother that I got close to was doing two life sentences, and he had been in this prison since 1959. I couldn't get over the fact that this gentleman had been there all these years. I didn't really get into what he did or how he did it. He just said he had two life sentences. He told me that since he was probably going to die in there and would never see the outside again, he would be really honored if I would wear a necklace he had made, on the rest of my journey, on the rest of my walk. He said it would give him a sense of being along with us if I took the necklace on the Walk. I told him I would be honored, and with that, he took it off his neck and gave it to me. I put it around my neck, shook his hand, and told him that I really appreciated him doing that, and that I would wear it on the rest of my journey across the United States.

After that, we talked with each other and had a real good gossip session. Bear Boy interrupted and said we were going to smoke the pipe and go into the Sweat Lodge. Everybody changed out of their clothes, wrapped the prison-issued towels around their waists, and went into the Sweat Lodge. We had a spiritual ceremony.

The prisoner that was keeping the stones hot, the Fire keeper, had the stones cooking for at least four hours, and we could see by the color of the stones that this was going to be a good one. They were amber/blue, and I said to Dennis and one of the inmates that it was going be a hot sweat, and they all said "Yeah, that's how we like 'em—HOT." There were roughly 25 to 30 people for this sweat, and we started to wonder how all of us were going to squeeze into the sweat lodge. But we had a double row, so we could hold a total of 32 people in all. We all knew that the more people there were in the sweat lodge the less air there would be to breathe, and that meant that the sweat would be that much hotter. I prepared myself and asked Creator to make me strong. Something just told me that these boys were going to run a hot sweat just to see how strong we were.

Bear Boy, the Medicine Man, was praying hard for all the prisoners, and the walkers were praying hard for the prisoners, and the prisoners were praying hard for the walkers to have a safe journey. This was one of the hottest sweats I had ever been in. With each person saying the prayer they wanted the other people to hear, this sweat wound up going eight rounds without a break. Although we didn't get to leave the Sweat Lodge, we did have some water between some of the rounds, and this made it somewhat easier. After all, we were in there for the pain and suffering, to sacrifice ourselves to the Creator to make us stronger.

We all knew from the get-go that this wasn't going to be an easy sweat. We all got through it, and as we came out of the Sweat Lodge we shook each other's hands, and thanked each other for the prayers and the good sweat that we had. We all drank plenty of water rather quickly, and appreciated the fact that we had been able to sweat with our Indian brothers.

We laid around on the grass, relaxing and talking. Our Indian brothers in prison wished we didn't have to go, so we could have another round in the sweat lodge. We couldn't go in for another round, but that particular sweat had left me pretty sluggish and tired for the rest of the day. It was a comfort to be out in the fresh air.

We stayed for six hours, and at the end of the day a guard came to us and said we would have to leave in 20 minutes. With that, we exchanged addresses with the Indian brothers that wanted to, said our good-byes, and got ready to leave the same way we came in—in formation. We told the Indian brothers that the road we would be walking would bring us by the prison in two days. The road was about a half mile from the prison, and we figured we would be going past around 3:00 in the afternoon. They said they would make it a point to be in the exercise yard, wearing headbands so we could see them, and we told them that we would wave back from the road to acknowledge them. They would be looking forward to that. That would make them feel that they were a part of the walk.

On our way out of the Colorado State Penitentiary the guard joked with us and said he hoped that none of the walkers decided to change clothes with any of the inmates. He started laughing, didn't think so. The guard wished us a pleasant journey, and thanked us for coming out to visit with the Indian prisoners. We loaded up into the van for our 30-mile journey back to the church, to join up with our second family.

We got back to the church, and the rest of the walkers and the people who lived there were all very anxious to find out how our visit and the sweat had gone with the prisoners. We could tell them nothing but the truth-it went very well. We were all thankful that the Creator had let us into the prison system to meet with our Indian brothers and we were real happy that everything had gone more than perfect. I was glad I was able to get in after not signing up. It was a joke between Dennis Banks and me that we would pass back and forth, now and then. He would say "Hey Harry, feel like sneaking into a prison today? Are you bored?" That would give me a laugh, and sometimes I needed it. My morale would be somewhat on the down side occasionally, because not everything was happy-go-lucky when I was walking everyday. Sometimes I just wanted to be by myself. Sometimes I found myself getting away from the whole walk and taking walks by myself to pray to the Creator and meditate. It did me a lot of good and helped me along my way to spend time by myself. Being the type of person that I am, I almost feel like I **have** to get off by myself every once in a while and pray to the Creator. It keeps me going. It keeps me strong. It keeps me spiritually fit.

After the sweats and all the feasting, everybody went into their tents or where ever they were sleeping, and got ready to move out of the church. We would be continuing our journey east, across Colorado, and I was looking forward to that. I was also looking forward to walking past the prison and waving to our Indian Brothers, keeping our word. I knew we would be down that way in another day and a half or so.

We kept walking, and the Colorado scenery made the days go by quickly. As we had promised, we got close to the area of the Colorado State Penitentiary and a few of the walkers took it upon themselves to carry some small hand held drums. We would be singing a prayer song when we walked past the prison and, hopefully, our Indian Brothers would be able to hear them. We were about half an hour away, and we took a break to prepare.

As we neared the prison, we saw a sign on the road that said "Prison Area- No Hitchhiking Allowed". We all kind of chuckled and said there ain't nobody hitchhiking out here, but we sure the hell are walking. We walked a little further and we could see the tops of the barbwire and double fences. It gave us butterflies. As we got closer we could see red banners waiving back and forth. There were roughly 30 to 50 Indian people and other people waving to us. I thought to myself, "Man, I know people over there. I was just there." I raised the Staff I was carrying to say "Hi" to them so they would know we could see them. The people were drumming and singing a prayer song, and we were hoping they could hear us. We knew they could see us because we could see them. We had kept our promise as we marched by the prison. I felt I had left a part of me there since I had been there two days earlier sweating with these Indian brothers. In my heart and mind, it felt good to know we had shared a small amount of time with these men. I just kept looking back until the prison faded out of sight.

The church we stayed in was very good to us. They put us up for four days. It was similar to what happened to us earlier at the University. We would get shuttled to where we had stopped walking the day before, and at the end of the day we would be shuttled back to the church. We made ourselves at home and they took very good care of us. Good home cooked church meals, and we loved ever minute of our stay.

After the four days, we saged off, left five people behind to clean up after us, and went on our way to Pueblo, Colorado. When we arrived in Pueblo, a note had been faxed to us saying that the church was the cleanest it had ever been, and the people we left behind did a fabulous job, which they always did. Every time we left a place that offered us shelter, we never had one complaint. No one ever said that they wished they hadn't let those Indians stay there because they left it really dirty. We were always proud of this and we wanted to stick by it. We wanted the word to get out that there were no problems, in case these places ever needed to be used again on a future walk.

We were making sure that the people on any future walk would more than likely be accepted into the church communities that had shelter, due to the fact that we had left a good impression.

We were all glad to move on down the road to a new spot, though, because it let us know we were making progress. We heard we would be staying at the fair grounds in Pueblo, in an inside shelter.

As I mentioned earlier, I would be meeting my wife in Colorado Springs for a love rendezvous. It had been a month or so since I had seen her and I missed her very much. The anticipation kept me going for two more days of walking. It kind of recharged me, and kept me in the best spirits I had been in for a while. Although I was never in a real bad mood, I had my mood swings just like everybody else. When I was in a good mood, I mentally took advantage of it, and it made my day go much better.

We finally got to Pueblo and made our way to the state fair grounds. It was a place to stay, out of the snow and the rain, although it wasn't heated. We all made do with what we were fortunate enough to have for free. I called my wife and she said she would be flying in. I had been anticipating this for two weeks. I was going to get Dave Patton in one of the support vehicles to drive me over to the airport in Colorado Springs and drop me off.

I was excited and anxious to see my wife, and when he dropped me off I started looking for Gate 120 where her flight would be coming in. It felt good to be around all these different people so I could do some "people watching" and check out how busy the airport was. I had almost forgotten that there were places like this with masses of people at one time. It kind of surprised me after walking all these months. I had my mind so focused on walking I had forgotten about the fast pace everybody kept. I got a chair and waited for my wife's flight to come in. I sat back and relaxed, reading a People Magazine.

I had been waiting about 45 minutes when they announced that flight 227 would be landing in a few minutes. I felt butterflies in my stomach, knowing soon we'd be together. I watched the plane pull up to the terminal, and got even more excited than I was before. She got off the plane after about five minutes. Man did she look good! It is very difficult to describe the feeling of holding her in my arms again, but let's just say that it made everything right. It all seemed worthwhile.

We rented a car and went to the Holiday Inn and made reservations for two days. We started the evening out in a very relaxing way. We got room service, soaked in the hot bath together, and just enjoyed each other's company. We watched cable TV, and it was almost fun to have that remote in my hand. We went to sleep, and the next morning we got a map of Colorado and took off in our rental car.

We went to the downtown area to a mall and shopped around. We had dinner and took in a movie. All in all, we were just happy to see each other, because we are very close. The day was almost gone and I knew that I only had one more day with my wife.

After today I wouldn't be seeing her until the midway point, which was Kansas City. Dennis had suggested that anyone who could afford it should drive or fly back home and get re-energized at the halfway point, and spend time with their family. But, they should be back on the ninth day, because on the tenth day, the camp that was set up in Kansas City would be leaving.

If you got there on the tenth day, no one would be in the camp and you would have some catching up to do. The other walkers and myself could make some really good time, and you just didn't want to get left behind. During the ten-day break, if there was any chance I could fly back home to Vegas I would do it. But if I didn't, then I would stay in the tent for ten days and **that** would be my midway break. If that happened, I would not be seeing my wife for almost three and a half months, until the walk was over. So, we spent the time we had real close, and enjoyed everything we did together. We had a real good two-day visit.

We got back to the airport and said our emotional good-byes. I told her to hold the fort down and I would stay in contact through letter and phone, which I was really good at doing. I could see the pain on her face, knowing she had to bear the burden of keeping us afloat by herself. Even though Karen is a strong woman, she can be fragile emotionally. She has had to be strong for both of us and rely on leaning on herself until this walk was over. I thanked the Creator for watching over her while I was gone.

With our good-byes, she got on the plane and I told her I would either see her in another month on our break, or I'd be seeing her after July 15th, when the walk was officially over.

I called Dave Patton back at the campsite in Pueblo. Being the good guy he is, he drove thirty-something miles back into Colorado Springs and picked me up at the airport and took me back to the campsite.

After spending two days at the Holiday Inn being pampered and massaged by my wife and just having a good old time, I knew I had to psyche myself up and get back into the swing of things. I had to get used to things again, like the discomfort of not having some of the luxuries I had had in the last two days. I would have to learn to go without again. I had no problem doing that. I got back to the fairgrounds and got my bedroll and my backpack, said "Hi" to everyone, and went to sleep.

The next morning we got up to the Rooster crow and had our breakfast. We had our morning circle and Dennis Banks told us we were going to walk a relatively short 18 miles that day. He made sure that everyone was doing alright, and he then announced that it was Tim's (one of the walkers) birthday. He asked Ava, who was from Switzerland, to sing Happy Birthday to him in her native language. So, with a red face she came to the center of the circle. They both got quite embarrassed, but it was all in fun. Everybody clapped their hands, and she fell back into the circle. Dennis also mentioned that anyone who usually wore headphones would not be allowed to do so, due to the area we were going into. There was a lot of traffic, and they didn't want anyone to get hit by a truck. With a few gripes and complaints, everybody agreed not to wear their headsets. We saged off, got in formation, and headed down the road, leaving Pueblo, Colorado, behind.

We were about 10 minutes into the walk and a car full of people pulled up and asked to sign our petition for executive clemency for Leonard Peltier. I told them the person in the support vehicle in back of us had the petition and they would have to go to them to sign. We found out later these people left about $100 worth of food and $100 in cash to help support our walk. We were very happy about that, as usual. It was people like this that helped us get to our next town, or even to our next state. If we hadn't come across people like this throughout the Walk, there would have been days when we would have been walking on an empty stomach. The Walk had been well planned, and Creator took care of the rest. So we were real grateful to the Creator for sending people like this our way.

We had been walking for about three hours and had gotten out of the heavy traffic, onto a country road. We were walking our usual brisk place when I looked down at the side of the road and saw a large black and white Hawk. I raised the Staff, stopped, and told everyone we had to respect this Hawk and sage it off. We formed a circle, saged off the hawk, and wrapped it in an old blanket. I told someone to put it in a support vehicle. Since I had found it, this would be my hawk, to do what I wanted with the feathers. I thanked the Creator for giving us this Hawk so we could sage it off and respect it, then have it's feathers to give to the walkers, or to add to the Staff, or to make what we wanted. Later, I would give one wing to Dave Patton, and one of the tail feathers to one of the walkers named Dukes. He was the Treasurer. He was the one that kept all the money in order. I kept the rest of the bird to add on to some Indian regalia that I had been making back home.

Throughout the day, people were stopping and asking to sign our petition, and they were honking and beeping. By this time, all the media coverage we had over the last two months was finally paying off. We were glad to see this, because we knew the word was out, and that was the main purpose of the Walk. After walking 18 miles that day, we had our usual evening circle, and saged off. Everybody felt good. Dennis Banks had an announcement from Carter Camp. He had been involved at Wounded Knee and various other Indian movements, and he sent Dennis a letter that was picked up that day at the post office. The letter asked if we could go out of our way a hundred and some miles (which would actually be over 200 miles-100 there and 100 back) into Oklahoma to hear his grievances, and his tribe's grievances. They would like to make the Walk for Justice aware of what was going on in the area, and they wanted us to take their message to Washington, D.C. with us.

Dennis, asked us if we would be willing to go 200 miles out of our way.   Instead of walking the intended 3,600 miles, we would be adding another 200 miles, which would make it 3,800, if we chose to go into Oklahoma and support the Ponca Tribe.   We decided to do it, and we were glad and thankful that we did.   It was one more state I could say I had been in.   It wasn't a very bad walk because we knew we didn't have to walk across the whole state.   We were right above Oklahoma in Kansas, so you could say it was just a hop, skip, and a jump.   We walked for a couple of days in rainy weather and hailstorms, and it was very cold.   A few people almost got hypothermia. I got very cold myself, and we had to stop several different times to warm up so we could walk the rest of the distance.   We took turns warming up in one of the Winnebago campers that had joined the walk two days earlier.

After that day of walking, which was 28 miles, we had our circle, and Dennis Banks told us we would be going to Sand Creek to honor our dead Indian Brothers and Sisters.   Anybody who wanted to go would load up into support vehicles and go.   Of course, I wanted to go there.   We would go the next day, after we finished our designated miles.

At Sand Creek, one hundred and fifty men, women, and children, of the Cheyenne Tribe were massacred by Colonel J.M. Chivington and his Colorado Volunteer Amy.   The massacre took place at the Indian campsite, and it caused such an outcry that Colorado statehood was delayed by more than a decade. Dennis Banks told us at the circle that we were going to take a non-scheduled day off and drive out to Sand Creek.

After the walk that day about 30 walkers got into support vehicles and went out to have a ceremony. It was very moving and emotional. I could just imagine how it might have looked back then. Today, it was a grassy meadow with about eight trees of medium size, black, with no leaves. They had kind of a ghostly look to them. At a drum ceremony we said prayers for about an hour, and wondered how it might have been. What was going through the minds of the Cheyenne when this all happened. It really made me feel sad to be where this took place, and I was glad that we were able to pay our respects to our fallen ancestors.

We loaded back up into the support vehicles and went back to the campsite, where we were taking the day off from walking. That was good, because after we saw where the massacre had taken place, after we saw where hundreds of our ancestors had fallen, we really didn't feel like getting back out onto the road and letting the thoughts and images slip away. They needed to be pondered.

From what I had seen of Colorado, I liked it the most. And that included the people we had met up to this time. The country was beautiful. I saw a lot of Bald Eagles and Golden Eagles. The wildlife and the scenes were very panoramic, and it was overwhelming to see all the pristine beauty. So far, it was the highlight of all the states we had been in. I had grown rather fond of Colorado.

I took a lot of pictures throughout the trip, and Colorado was the state where I used my camera the most. It was time to continue on our journey leading into Kansas.

"Colorado, you are beautiful!"

KANSAS

Driving through Kansas can get monotonous. Walking in Kansas can put you to sleep. It's not a bad place; in fact it is very historical. When you read books about the Old West, or you watch some of the westerns at the movies or on TV, there is a good chance that the events you are learning about took place in Kansas.
I'm not trying to say anything bad about Kansas. However, when you are walking an endless ribbon of asphalt, watching the heat rise and making everything on the horizon look like a scene from the movie High Plains Drifter, then you can think of a lot of other places you'd rather be. The land is flat, and it stretches out for miles and miles. The only thing to see

was an occasional dust devil, kicking up dirt and sand and swirling it all around, sometimes all around us. It is amazing to think about 130 years ago buffalo herds roamed these very plains in vast numbers, they were walking commissaries and were referred to as 'Uncle' by the Plains Indians, due to all the items of sustenance they provided. This is a way of life which is gone forever. I found my mind wandering, thinking back to an earlier mission that I had been on.

In 1972, word was circulating that there was going to be a caravan to D.C. This turned out to be known as "The Take Over of the Bureau of Indian Affairs building". I was involved in that seven-day takeover. I was there with Marge Stevens and Ronnie Hill. Leonard Peltier worked in the same office that I worked in and I had become acquainted with him. He was also at the B.I.A. takeover. So was Dennis Banks, Russell Means, Leonard Crowdog, and many others. The takeover consisted of seizing and occupying the building. We had several pow wows, right inside the building, with high profile news media coverage. Records were taken out of the B.I.A., and I was told that they were later buried on one of the reservations out in Wisconsin.

The FBI was really mad about this, because they had no access to any of the records. With no records they didn't really know what they owned or what they had. They were really pissed.

I was hoping everything would go real smooth at the B.I.A. because I was not ready to go back to prison for the third time. But I figured I had to do what I had to do. Whatever was best for my people. The law had the building surrounded for seven days. Dennis Banks, Russell Means, and Clyde Bellecourt were the spokespersons. They were the ones the media did all the talking to. I was just Harry Kindness, and no one knew me except the people I worked with back in Wisconsin. We were all amazed at how the news media was listening to the three of them, and seemed to be paying attention. They were our leaders and our chiefs as far as we were concerned.

The authorities gave us a deadline everyday as to when we had to be out of the B.I.A., but everyday the deadline was extended. Since it was an election year for President Nixon they did not want the media to run with this story and let the whole world know that the American Indian Movement had taken over the Bureau of Indian Affairs Building. They didn't want to have a massacre, of blood or ink, and they were keeping it as quiet as possible. What they did do, was agree to pay us money. Money was distributed to all the Indians involved with the B.I.A. takeover. Everyone received the money necessary to get back home. I was given money to get on a Greyhound Bus and go back home to Wisconsin.

It was great to get out of there without an arrest. I got home almost three days later and went back to work at A.I.M. in Milwaukee. We gossiped about the seven-day takeover, it was a big deal to everyone.

A few days later I was at home after work and there was a knock at the door. I didn't have a peephole, so I yelled through the door to find out who it was. The answer was "FBI". I asked what they wanted, and they said they just wanted to talk to me. I opened the door and invited them in. They let me know that they knew I worked for A.I.M. and that I was involved in the B.I.A. takeover. I asked them how they knew and they said that someone saw me there, so I knew that there must have been an insider, an informant that was giving names. I asked them if they had a picture of me being there. They said no, but **they** knew I was there, and **I** knew I was there. I told them I wasn't, and my girlfriend at the time provided me with an alibi, saying that we were in the State Park for eight days on a camping trip. They couldn't prove that I was there, but they said that they would get back to me when they came up with more proof. I never did hear any more from them.

My next involvement as an activist came a year later, during the 71-day siege at Wounded Knee. I was involved on three of those days, and knowing that the FBI was watching me made me apprehensive. But I did run ammunition, food and guns up to my people at Wounded Knee. I was very glad to have participated, even though I was only there for three out of the 71 days. I am **proud** to say I was at the takeover of the B.I.A. and the siege at Wounded Knee. A person can only take, and take for so long. There comes a time when you have to **do** something. That was my time.

I hadn't really been involved in anything else since then, up to the present time. Which brings me back to the Walk for Justice. I can truthfully say that my involvement in the movement has lasted for those 22 years, and here I was, on the Walk for Justice for Leonard Peltier. It's my time again, to **do** something.

I am glad this wasn't a violent demonstration like the others. It was a spiritual walk. I didn't have to worry about being thrown into jail. But if it had been a violent protest I would have been there, because I believe strongly in the American Indian Movement beliefs. The Movement is more important than any one individual. Separating the people from their Chiefs had not worked before, and it would not work now. We are a proud people, and we are still strong.

On the other hand, I was glad that A.I.M was being run a little different. There were no guns, no alcohol, and no drugs on this Walk. It was strictly a spiritual walk to bring the spotlight back on Leonard Peltier's case, and for the 14 other reasons as well. I will always be an A.I.M. member because I believe in what we do and have done, and how we have helped our people out for the last 26 years. After all, my belief in Leonard Peltier's innocence and A.I.M. is what got me on the walk, taking me away from my home, family, and friends. It is what brought me here, to my new friends all across the country, and to my second family. It is what gave me the will to go on every day. It is what gave my wife the strength to hold down the fort while I was gone and support me 100%. I am in A.I.M. for life.

My mind came back from the past to the present, and we were still in Kansas. But we wouldn't be for long. It was time to take our detour into Oklahoma, and put another state under our belts.

Kansas, we'll be back.

OKLAHOMA

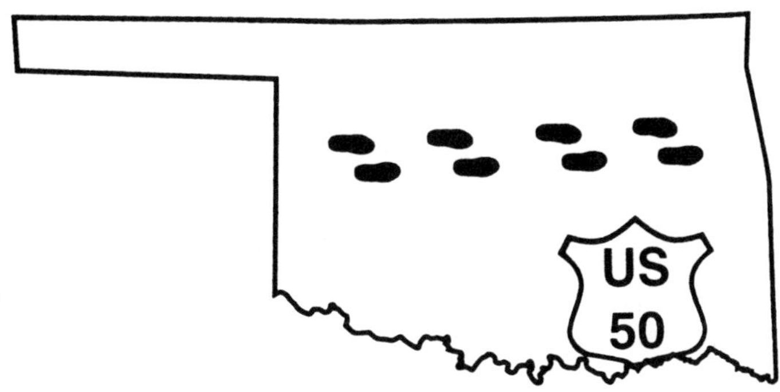

After walking for almost three days in Oklahoma, we got onto the Ponca Tribe Reservation, where Carter Camp met us. I did not know him, so I was glad to meet him and other tribe members. I was very excited because I had never even heard of the Ponca Tribe. I expected them to look different, probably because of the name Ponca. It kind of threw me off.

Anyway, 80 people from the tribe came out to meet us, set up a camp, and prepare a feast for us. They were proud and very supportive of the Walk for Justice. We had a drum ceremony and feasted until about midnight. In the morning we would be going onto the reservation, where we would have a talk and find out what they wanted us to know. Our meeting would be held in an old school house.

So, after all the feasting, Dennis Banks made us aware of what was going to happen the next day. After his talk we went to bed, because we had to get up at eight the next morning. I promptly fell asleep.

The next thing I knew, we were all in circle. We saged off, then got ready and went to the schoolhouse. The meeting lasted about an hour and a half, after a drum ceremony.

The main concern of the Ponca Tribe was what the government wanted to do in the area. They were trying to build a nuclear waste dump on the reservation, and Carter and 90% of the rest of the tribe did not want it to happen.

This was the main issue. Only one person had signed an agreement saying they would accept the nuclear dump. They found out that this person had been offered a large sum of money to sign the paper. The nuclear waste company was trying to say that the agreement had been signed, and they were going to put the dump here.

Carter said "No you won't, you're not going to put a dump here, because it takes more than one signature."

He told them they needed the whole tribal council's consent. But, the nuclear waste company felt one signature was good enough. So, the main purpose of our going out of our way was to let the people in Washington, D.C. know about this, by adding it to our list of grievances.

The Walk For Justice was not just for Leonard Peltier. It was about injustice in other areas concerning Indians. We had to be heard and make people realize what was happening on native land was not right or just. For some reason these companies and government agencies seem to think they are separate from places that get nuclear waste dumped. But that waste will effect them, sooner or later. It will hurt the Ponca people, but then the next generation of people will be effected. Then the wind and rain will carry that waste, eventually, to all those that thought it was okay to put it there. If they would only realize they are destroying their home, as well as the home they forced native people to stay on.

We were not going to let this dump be forced onto the Ponca Tribe Reservation. We already knew what our stand was on nuclear dumping on Native lands. We are totally opposed to it, and we weren't going to let it be forced onto the reservation land without a fight. The Ponca people had been forced off their homeland and placed here in Oklahoma, and now the government wanted to take that land to put in a nuclear dump that no one else wanted in their backyard.

It was as if the government was saying, "Make the Indians take it. They won't say anything or do anything about it." Well, they were wrong. We were on a quest for justice.

We assured Carter and the rest of the tribe members that we would carry their grievance, and signed letter to take to Washington, D.C. with us. We would be presenting this to one of the Congressmen there.

Carter Camp and his family joined the Walk for Justice, and stayed with the walk, on and off, all the way to Washington, D.C.

KANSAS AGAIN

The Walk for Justice continued to trek through Kansas, with hardly anything to tell you about. The people were nice, but we were anxious to see something besides flat land. We still had about eight more miles to go this day, and we were about two days out of Kansas City. We finished the eight miles, and Dennis told me to call it a day, and told the rest of the walkers to set up camp. We formed a circle and saged off.

After the circle I went to see Dennis in his trailer, and I told him that since we were a little more than half way across the country, each day I walked was getting me a little closer to the Sundance at Pipestone, Minnesota in August. I told him I wanted his opinion as to how I could best prepare myself.

Dennis was a full-fledged Sundancer and I respected what he had to say.

I told him I had been planning on going to the Sundance for the past year. Rumor had it that he was in possession of four eagle-bone whistles, and I asked him for permission to use one of the eagle-bone whistles in the Sundance. That would put me one step closer to being ready. He told me that participating in the Sundance was not an easy thing. I told him that that was why I had come to him. He said it's a very hard ceremony, and he suggested I start out the next time we have a smaller mileage goal, like an 18-mile day versus 30 to 35, by walking the entire day without food or water. He said I should do this a few times during the remaining three months of the walk. He also told me that once I accepted that eagle bone whistle from him I was committing myself to dance at the Sundance. He told me to make sure that was what I wanted to do, and that my mind was set. I knew I was preparing myself by going on this spiritual walk. I knew I was ready and this was what I wanted to do. So, I told Dennis I would be honored if he would sponsor me for the Sundance, and I committed to him that I would be there. And I committed to Creator that I would be there for four years.

I would need a ceremonial dance skirt, so I went to his daughter, Glenda, right after I talked to Dennis to see if she would make it for me. I told her that Dennis had given me the eagle-bone whistle and I needed someone to make the ceremonial skirt. She said she gladly would. She said she would be honored. I thanked her, and I was **another** step closer to the Sundance, since I had these two sacred items. Because these two items had come my way, I had more power and more energy. I was looking forward to dancing for the people, for my family, and for myself. I wanted the time to go by fast. I wished it would take place the very next day.

In any case, it was back to walking. We entered Kansas on April 20 and we would be leaving on May 12, which was only two days away. The distance across Kansas was 450 miles. We broke camp the next morning and headed out for a 28 mile day. Everybody was in good spirits. We saged off and were on our way. It started to rain, and we really didn't mind because the weather was getting warmer. It rained for only half the day and then we were in for a treat. It got sunny and stayed above 70 degrees the rest of the day.

We were about eight miles into the walk when a news media van pulled up and came along side me. The gentlemen said they were from Missouri, and they were looking for the Walk for Justice. They said they wanted to speak to the spokesperson, Harry Kindness, and I told them that was me. However, I told them, I wouldn't be able to talk to them unless they wanted to ride along side me and stick the microphone out the window, because we weren't wasting any time and we had to make tracks. One of them told me to call him when I got across into Missouri, and he gave me his card. He was with the Chillicothe News Media and wanted to do an interview. I told him I would call him the day we got in.

A support vehicle pulled up with lunch, which consisted of peanut butter sandwiches and fruit that was made the night before. They also brought us water. We were sitting around on a grassy knoll and Dennis Banks told us to listen up. He said that the ones that aren't filling up their canteens in the morning had better start doing it. We started having problems with people sharing their canteens, and somebody had been passing the flu bug around. That is the main reason I didn't share my canteen with anybody. It may sound cold, but if somebody was real thirsty and didn't have any water I would tell them they should have filled up their canteen when they left in the morning. I told them I was sorry, but I didn't want to catch anything that was going around. Dennis stressed the fact that everyone should be filling their canteens in the morning, and he didn't want to hear any sniveling or whining if someone ran out of water. People started filling up their canteens. The flu bug subsided, and no one else got sick, other than having sore feet and a couple of colds. If anyone did get sick, they would ride in a support vehicle. Up to this point, no one got sick enough to go into a hospital or be taken off by an ambulance to the next county. We had a pretty fit bunch of walkers.

There was a bit of a health nut in me. I always took it upon myself to take my herbs and a good strong multi-vitamin every day. I had fallen into a routine over the last 20 years, and I considered myself to be in pretty good shape for 42 years old. It was almost May 10, and I hadn't been sick on the whole trip. I didn't have to stop due to sore feet, either, because of my investment in a very good pair of walking shoes. Although my feet and muscles were sore, and I did get blisters, I felt I was in better shape than anybody else on the walk.

Dennis would often tell me to save at least 10 miles for him because he would walk with the Staff everyday also. Most of the time, he was running the show, but he did his walking whenever he could. We always had a good time with him carrying the Staff next to me, with his sense of humor. He kept me entertained and I enjoyed his company very much. If he was within five feet of me he always had me laughing. This helped me a lot because I'm the type of person that likes to tell jokes and hear jokes. Along the way we would get into all kinds of conversation, and this helped to pass the time.

But you had to keep your mind on the walk to make sure you were able to jump in case a vehicle strayed over the line. You always had to be watching your back, and that's why the support vehicle was always behind me when I walked by myself in the morning. And, they always carried water and a lot of carbohydrates to keep me going. They were instrumental in keeping me from getting hit several times out on the road. Coming through the eastern portion of the country, people just seemed to drive a little crazier than they did back west. I was always looking over my shoulder because I had almost been hit a few times. I didn't want to end up with broken legs or have to end the walk due to carelessness, or someone's stupid driving. I was always on my toes, always watching. I stayed focused, and every so often a support vehicle would come up and tell me how far we had come and how far we had to go.

There was no music. I didn't need music because I had all the natural sounds to take in, and the wildlife to look at. Everybody got something out of the trip. There was always something going on. Somebody would see something somebody else didn't see and would bring it to everyone's attention. We were pretty much a happy bunch of walkers, and we all took care of each other and watched each other's back. We were one big family. We all got along pretty good. Any little arguments we had didn't amount to anything, and they weren't very serious. Personally, I think it went really well, considering all the different types of people, the different types of weather, and the day-to-day business that went along with walking.

Midway through the trip I had lost 20 pounds, and I was on my second pair of hiking boots. I knew I would need a third pair before I was finished. Just about the time I would get comfortable with a pair of boots I would have to get a new pair. My feet were in bad shape off and on, and I had some pretty big calluses built up. Some days it was harder than the day before, sometimes easier. We never knew how a day was going to go. We just had to keep at it, one foot in front of the other, one step at a time. As they say, "A journey of a thousand miles begins with one step". In our case it was 3,800 miles, but we still had to take that first step every day.

We were still in Kansas, and once again, my mind started on a journey of its own. It had been 22 years since I had last been in D.C., and it was under different circumstances. When we got to D.C. this time, we would be having a rally and a march to let everyone know why we had made the Walk and why we were there, which was seeking executive clemency for Leonard Peltier, and the other 15 causes. I was looking forward to getting there, under different circumstances this time. All in all, we were just glad to be close to the halfway mark.

Throughout the United States, with all the colleges Dennis Banks had spoken at, and all the interviews I had given on TV, radio and to the newspapers, the word was definitely getting out. Before we got to each state line the people knew we were coming, and they welcomed us. We got more and more coverage, and we were all happy about that. July 14th would be here before we knew it, and we wanted Washington, D. C. to know we were coming, so every newspaper article, every radio or TV interview helped prepare for that day.

Back to the reality of Kansas. At morning circle Dennis would tell us what to expect and how to speak for the American Indian Movement. Everyday we got fresh news, and it got better and better. It was great to know that we were out there walking and we had all that support. We would be entering Kansas City, Missouri on the 13th of May. It would take 266 miles to get us across Missouri.

The last two days of walking in Kansas were relatively easy. On that particular morning at the circle, Dennis Banks said he would be leaving to go into Washington, D.C., to help organize, and let people know about the walk coming on July 14th. He then told everyone he would be putting me in charge of the walk for the four days he would be gone. I was very honored by this, because it showed that he trusted me for leadership, to guide these people farther down the road. It was a real good feeling. Although no one was really a boss, somebody had to be in charge. And, since I was one of the Staff carriers, and a strong walker who had started from Alcatraz and walked the whole way, he just felt I would be the best person to leave in charge while he was gone. Dennis also asked if everyone was feeling all right, and asked if there was anyone who couldn't walk that specific day. If there were people who couldn't walk, they would have to get in a support vehicle. Sometimes these morning circles would last 10 minutes or longer. That particular morning we found out that one of the walkers was having a birthday, so for something different, Dennis asked the walkers from Japan to come out and sing Happy Birthday to A.A., our photographer from Switzerland. They sang Happy Birthday to her in Japanese. It sounded different to our ears, and it started our day out with laughter and humor. We saged off and were on down the road.

Our day started out as usual, with us all in formation and walking to the right side of the white line. We started with a moderate pace until everyone got somewhat warmed up and then we really got moving. We had only been walking about an hour, and at least five people pulled up to sign the Leonard Peltier petition.   It was good to have people walk up from out of nowhere and say "We saw you on the news". A lot more times than not they would leave donations of food and money. It always made our day go easier, knowing we had support, even from people we didn't know. We always looked forward to meeting new people, whether it was for three minutes, three hours, or three days. We would have occasional stops where we would find a country store, and I'd let everyone take a five-minute break. If it lasted longer, we would have to make it up by walking faster.

We would come across these really nice country stores that would have everything you would want to buy. We would buy a few select items that we could afford or needed, and everybody would get their sodas, potato chips or a sandwich. People were always very friendly in these country stores. Usually, they heard from other people that they would probably have these walkers coming through. They all welcomed us with open arms and were supportive of the cause. Many times they would sign our petition. I would also get in my five-minute call, and leave a message for my wife on the answering machine. I used to wonder how those little stores were able to make it out there. It was a real treat to come across these little places, and it made the break go a lot better.

We walked at a very brisk pace because everyone knew we only had one more day in Kansas. The 450 miles going across Kansas seemed longer than it did in Nevada, for some reason. I don't know why, but for some reason it did. We were all looking forward to the next day, which would be our last in Kansas. We were about five miles out from our next campsite when a news reporter jumped out of a van. We could see him down the road with all these cameras around his neck. As we approached he made sure we were the Walk for Justice. He said he was a news reporter from Kansas City and he had come out to cover the walk. He had been told that Harry Kindness was the spokesperson for the walk, and he wanted to speak with him. I told him that was me, and he asked to walk along side and interview me. I told him it was no problem, but I also told him I wouldn't be slowing my pace down, and he would have to keep up. He laughed and said no problem.

He asked me what tribe I was from and how long I had been on the walk. I told him Oneida, and from the starting point. He asked me my age, how many people we had, how many people had joined since the beginning, and what was the highest number of miles we had walked in one day. He was basically trying to get all the information he could. I felt kind of sorry for him because he had all that camera equipment on his body, so I tended to slow down a little bit. He was a little out of breath trying to interview me. I wasn't, because I was in condition from the last few months of walking, so I had no problem talking to him as we walked. He said, "I got to give up these cigarettes". I told him they'd kill him quicker than anything else, and he started laughing. He said, "Not before I finish this interview". We had a good interview, which lasted roughly 15 minutes. He said thanks a lot and he would get it into the next day's paper.

I wanted to make sure to pick up a copy and add it to the rest of the newspaper clippings I had been taking for myself. I was looking forward to getting that newspaper the next day and see how good an article the reporter did on us. Not long after the interview, Dave Patton drove up to the front of the walkers and told me we had another mile and we could stop for the day. We got that mile out of the way, and our day came to an end with the circle, thanking the Creator for giving us a safe walk. We saged off, and everybody broke away to set up their camping equipment after my brief talk. I didn't want to stand out there and give a long talk, because I felt Dennis Banks did it better than me. We would get up in the morning to complete our last day of walking through Kansas.

That morning we got up to the infamous Rooster call. We had all gotten used to it, and it would never be the same for anybody when morning came around, once this walk was over. In any case, he got the job done. We had the morning circle, with our gossip and grievances and anything else anybody would want to say.   Sometimes our circle would go on for 45 minutes, and we would have to cut it short and tell people if they have anything to complain about or specific problems, they would have to say it at the evening circle. In the morning we would have to get up and eat our breakfast and get going.

We were nearing the end of Kansas and were going to take another detour up to Leavenworth, Kansas. Home of the infamous federal prison where Leonard Peltier was incarcerated for the last 18 years.

Dennis Banks informed us that we would be having a demonstration on the front lawn of Leavenworth Penitentiary for the whole day. We were planning to face the cell block area where Peltier was rumored to be housed, so that he would hear the drum ceremony and singing of the A.I.M. song in commemoration of his unjust imprisonment.

A group of 150 people consisting of walkers, and area residents who supported the movement turned out along with the media who recorded the event which made front page headlines the next day.

The same day of the demonstration we were unaware that Peltier's Aunt came to visit him. Afterwards, she came out and addressed the A.I.M. members and supporters relaying Leonard's message to us. She told us that at the time of the drum ceremony the inmates in the cell block could hear the drums and they yelled, "Leonard your people are here for you." Leonard looked out his cell window and could see the crowd that had gathered in recognition of him, he then became very emotional and told his aunt to thank the supporters and A.I.M. for not forgetting about him.

After a long period of demonstration it was time to rest and prepare to move on.

Personally, it was never the first 10 or 15 miles of walking that bothered me. It was always the last five. The last five miles always seemed like 10 miles to me. For other walkers in the group it was the reverse.

Our last day in Kansas was good because it was only a 16-mile day. It seemed somewhat like a walk in the park. I figured since it was only a 16-mile day we would take our time and go at a slower pace. We got into our designated campsite, which was only one mile from the Missouri border.

Dennis Banks called back from D.C. and left a message for us. He wanted to know how things were doing, and if I was keeping things together. That night I asked everyone at the circle if I was being too rough on them. Were we doing good together without Dennis Banks being here? We were all looking forward to his return. After the circle I wrote a letter and went to bed in a real good mood, because I knew we had one more mile and we would be in Missouri. Everybody was really excited, knowing we were about to get one more state under our belts. I drifted off to sleep, and before I knew it, everybody was up to the Rooster call.

At the morning circle, I reminded everyone that Dennis would be back tomorrow and that we only had to walk a mile and we would be in Missouri. Our total mileage for the day would be 23 miles. After the circle, we were back on the white line. Kansas, you're a great state, but I am truly glad that you are behind me.

MISSOURI

It was May 13th, and we had just passed the sign that said, "Welcome to Missouri". I had been in Missouri for less than a half-hour, when the reporter who had come out to meet us in Kansas hooked up with me. He was from a Chillicothe radio station. This is how the interview went:

<u>Interviewer</u>: This group is about 70 people strong. What was the main focus in getting this Walk started?

<u>Harry</u>: The whole thing was, and still is, Leonard Peltier's imprisonment for almost 19 years. The only way he can be released from prison, where we consider him a POW, is by executive clemency. All his legal avenues have been exhausted. We're hopeful that President Clinton and Hillary will grant that executive clemency. When he had his appeal last year, the DA who tried him 18 years ago stood up, and in

the 8th circuit appellate court admitted that the FBI really didn't know **who** shot the two FBI agents. The judge who was hearing the case asked him what he meant, and that kind of gave us the green light to say something's not right. We haven't forgotten about him and the Walk has been focused around his release.

Interviewer: This is apparently something that happened on a reservation.

Harry: That's right. It was in South Dakota, on the Oglala Reservation in 1975. Leonard Peltier was accused of killing two FBI agents and sentenced to two life terms in the Leavenworth Penitentiary, where he has been to this date. We stopped by the prison before we got to Kansas City. He heard us, and was well aware that we were outside the prison supporting him.

Interviewer: This is obviously something, going coast to coast, that is drawing a lot of national attention. Is this one of the bigger things A.I.M. has done to try and draw attention to your cause?

Harry: Yeah, I would have to say they had "The Longest Walk" in 1978 and that was a success. Both walks are similar, but we have other issues in addition to the 1978 walk. That was a successful walk and we're hopeful this walk will be the same.

Interviewer: Once again, if you have just joined us, Harry Kindness of the American Indian Movement is our guest this morning. Mr. Kindness is with the Walk for Justice. What time are you shoving off on Thursday morning?

Harry: I believe 8:00 o'clock in the morning. We average 35 miles a day, and we have a mile marker that we set out for. When we come to that, we stop. We have covered some 1900 miles, up and over the Rocky Mountains. We have endured all types of weather-blizzards, rain storms, tornadoes. Everybody came through fine and dandy with the exception of sore feet.

Interviewer: Of course, by the time our listeners are hearing this taped interview, you've already started on your trek east. When you talk about issues facing the American Indian Movement, help us, because there are many of us that do not know what you are talking about. I suppose it has always been the assumption that on reservations you have complete control. But, I know you're looking for fishing rights. Where are we missing out on some information?

Harry: To make a long story short, up in Wisconsin, we have a fishing rights issue. The Indians on the reservation need the fishing time to gather food for their families. The fishermen that come up there at that time of year do it strictly for sport. Our treaty rights let us spear fish first. They feel that we're getting a right that should belong to them, too. They claim we get all the trophy fish and we "over spear". But it's all regulated, and that's not the case. They have to realize that that's putting food in the stomachs of our Indian families, and that's a whole different issue, versus putting a walleye on the wall and looking at it as a trophy. They don't like it, but it was a treaty that was signed, and it's one of the few treaties the

U.S. government has lived up to. We're not ready to give it away, sell it, or let them buy the rights to fish anytime they want.

Interviewer: Has that gone to court?

Harry: Yes, it has. It was shot down, but other people are trying to reopen it. Of course, they're not satisfied with that issue. But we're going to make sure nothing negative comes of it on our end.

Interviewer: What other issue is A.I.M. trying to draw attention to?

Harry: Nuclear waste sites out west. They're making all this nuclear waste and they have to store it somewhere, but nobody wants it. More or less, the government is saying we're going to pay you to put this waste on your reservations. Well, we don't want it. In fact, they don't want to stop making it. They don't have any place to put it. Ask the people in Washington if they want to put it in the back yard of the White House. We don't want it and we're not accepting it. In a round about way, they're already saying we don't have a choice. When that goes into the ground, it affects all people. We've got to stop the raping of Mother Earth. Eighty years ago you could drink out of the lakes and rivers. Now, everybody's drinking bottled water. That's only one of the examples. I'm sure all races, no matter who they are, aren't happy about some of the things going on with nature. We're not trying to get people to live like Indians, we just want people to respect Mother Earth and try to come in focus with what some people are doing to destroy it. Everybody can help and try to get it back on the right track.

<u>Interviewer</u>: There's been a lot in the news, I think one particular case on the East Coast, maybe Massachusetts if I'm not mistaken, where many of the Indians on reservations are willing to bring in Casino Gambling as a way of generating revenue. Is this any issue you're involved in?

<u>Harry</u>: We don't consider that an issue. It's a positive for the American Indian because it's putting money on the reservations. We're building clinics and schools. That money is going to positive causes. It's self-supporting. We welcome other races to work on the reservations in the Casinos. It's not like we're saying, well, this is Indian land and they're our Casinos, and we don't want white people here. We're not a racist culture. We just want to be treated as equals and we do the same. The Staff that we carry on the journey has eagle feathers on it and we follow it. That Staff has a red ribbon, white ribbon, black ribbon, and yellow ribbon, and that represents all races. We carry that Staff for all races and to show unity. We want everyone to live as one. It is an A.I.M. march and the issues are American Indian issues, but they affect everyone. We walk for all peoples.

<u>Interviewer</u>: We talked a lot about the reservations and the things in relation to the United States keeping it's treaties that were signed many years ago. Do you have any idea what percentage of American Indians live on reservations compared to those that do not?

127

<u>Harry</u>: Well, to the best of my knowledge, there are reservations in just about every state, with the exception of Missouri. You have people that were born and raised on a reservation. Some live there and some die there, but some of them leave and become urban Indians. We come to the city and find employment, or we don't. A good percentage wind up back on the reservation because there's prejudice out there. A lot of us leave our custom of long hair and various other customs that people don't have an insight on, either out of ignorance or just indifference. It's big step to take if you've been living on a reservation most of your life. As far as percentages, only the B.I.A. knows that. We have tribal counts, which tell how many people are on the reservations. I could only guess.

<u>Interviewer</u>:   Help us to understand how the reservation is run. Is that ruled by a Tribal Council?

<u>Harry</u>: There is a Tribal Council and you have the B.I.A. Everybody has a hand in regulating the goings on. All the people have a say. We bring everything to the people and the people bring it to the council. If somebody doesn't think we're doing it right, or somebody doesn't like the B.I.A., we're the first to know. It's all federal, and the FBI does get involved in matters, whether they're right or wrong.

<u>Interviewer</u>: You may be new to this community, but there's a tremendous fascination in our area because we've had such a rich history with the Native American Indians, and I know you folks are always

welcome when you come here. We have a feast that is held here every year and Indians visit from all over the country. Maybe it's place you can visit with us in years to come.

<u>Harry</u>: Oh definitely. I can see the hospitality and the friendliness and openness we have received in the short time we have been here. I'm very pleased with the hospitality people have shown us. I'm sure I speak for everybody else.

I enjoyed this interview. He seemed genuinely interested in the Leonard Peltier case.

He was very sincere, and I thought the interview went well. We were glad it was a high profile radio station, and it would be going out to many of the states we had been in, and to some of the states we were going to. It was May 13th, and we had 266 miles to go. We would be in Missouri until the 26th of May.

After the interview we picked up the pace because we had taken an unscheduled break. That was no problem. We were in our seventh state and everybody was happy that Dennis Banks would be returning, so we were able to step lively. In the short time that we had been in Missouri we could see signs that it wasn't going to be as friendly a state as some of the others. We had heard that St. Louis was somewhat racial and redneck. This is only what we had heard, but we were only in the state about an hour before we came into contact with our first racial slur. A bunch of teenage kids screamed out the window of their car, "Why don't you f-----g Indians go back where you belong!" I asked Dale VanFleet what did they mean by, "Go back where you belong?" I told him that it was the other way around. <u>This</u> is where **we were from**. I told myself, "I don't even need to waste my time thinking about ignorant people like that."

About five miles into the walk, the police stopped us and asked us what it was about. The police told us we would have to walk on the sidewalk while passing through their area. We had a permit to walk in the street, but the cop was kind of a redneck, so I told everybody to walk on the sidewalk so we wouldn't have any trouble. I could tell this wasn't going to be easy. Less than two hours into the state, we already had two encounters. We didn't like that feeling, but it was something we would have to get used to. We found the people in Missouri to be very cold, and a lot of negativity was coming our way. On our lunch break I told everyone to just take it easy, and the faster we walked, the faster we would get through this state. For this day we had designated 31 miles. We did get some positive waves, though, and some people did sign our petition. We figured we just had to take the bad with the good.

The temperature was around 82 degrees, and we had to stop for extra water along the way. We camped about dusk and discussed what had happened that day, around the circle. We all agreed it was good that we only had to go 266 miles to get out of the state. It wasn't as though it was a long state, like Nevada. We went about our business, and I called my wife. I told her we were in our seventh state, and she told me that members of my family had seen a story about us on the news. I turned in and went to bed a short time later, thinking how good it would be to kiss Karen goodnight.

It was hot and muggy when I got up. It was going to be a hot day for walking. At morning circle I told everyone to act like adults if anyone yells anything. We broke camp, cleaned up our area, and walked out of there for our second day in Missouri. We walked for a long time with no troubles and everyone was in good spirits. Later in the day, a car pulled up and asked who the man in charge was. I didn't want to go into the deal about how nobody was really in charge, so I said "You could say I am." He told me he was the manager of the McDonald's about a half-mile down the road and he wanted to give us lunch for free. We all got what we wanted at McDonald's, and we thanked them. I felt like, well, maybe there were good people in Missouri after all.

Our target walk for the day was 27 miles, and we lost a little time because we were in the city where we had to cross streets and wait for lights. We were going to be camping at a state park. Little did I know that we would be having an encounter with the Missouri police. It was a rough walk for everybody because of the heat and humidity, but we finally got to our campsite and got everything set up. We would be spending two days here and all day we were expecting Dennis Banks' return. But instead, we got a call that said he would be staying in Washington an additional two days. We were a little disappointed, but we knew he was doing what needed to be done, so we could do what **we** had to do.

I set up my tent. The park had something like a museum of old farm buildings and equipment everywhere. It was all free, and you could take your own little personal tour. There were around 10 different buildings and it was an old army facility. It was well known that this was the last place soldiers stayed before they went to fight the hostile Indians.

The next morning, I wanted to go shopping, but I was first going to learn as much as I could about this place. I went through the individual buildings by myself, and I noticed a park ranger in his vehicle. He was staring me down, and he didn't have the nice look of hospitality. I went into the old cavalry building and then was on my way to the horse stable when I noticed the Ranger's car was gone, but I didn't think anything of it. When I was on my way to the third building I heard somebody say "Hey, you!" It was the Park Ranger. I was kind of surprised that he was still watching me. When he asked me what I was doing, I asked him what he meant, then told him I was taking a tour of the facility. He said they didn't want me going in the buildings. I looked over to the car and noticed he had another person with him now. I got a little concerned. I told him the sign said it was open to the public from 9:00 to 5:00. He got out of the car with a real attitude and told me he knew what the sign said, and he didn't want me in the building. I said this is a public place and all I want to do is go in the building and finish my tour. At this point, he unholstered and pulled his gun on me. He told me he wanted to see some ID, and told me to "stop f---ing talking back to him".

I was totally lost for words. He wanted to know who I was in the park with, and what I was doing. I told him I was taking a tour of the buildings. At this point, the other walkers saw what was going on and they came over. The Rangers got a little nervous and told me to tell them to go away. About 10 walkers came over and the Rangers told them to go away. I told the walkers that everything was fine and they should go back to the campsite. This made the Rangers feel like I was "obeying" them. He told me he didn't want to see me in these buildings and if I went in I would be arrested. I didn't understand it and I took it as outright harassment, but I didn't want things to get out of hand. I didn't want any of us to get arrested, so I told him I would leave. It took me most of the day to get over it. I wanted to go into the buildings anyway, but I didn't. Maybe Dennis would have handled it different, and maybe he wouldn't.

During the two days we were there, the Rangers continually circled our camp and kept an eye on us. At the daily circles, I told everyone to keep cool, and I kept reminding them that Dennis would be back in a day or two.

I went into town and did some shopping, and talked to my wife on the phone. That night we had a drum ceremony and were singing some of our spiritual songs. During the night we heard honking, and what sounded at first like gunshots, but then we realized that someone was throwing firecrackers. We heard people yelling, "Get the F—k outta here!" - another negative encounter. I figured it was either going to get worse or get better, and I sure hoped it would get better. Everyone went back to sleep and I got two volunteers, Felipe who was a martial arts expert, and Bruce Dorman, to stand watch. They did it in shifts. In the morning I asked them what had happened during the night and they said that people drove through and put their brights on the campsite. At the morning circle I told everyone that since it was daylight we didn't have to worry. We knew we weren't welcome here, so we saged off, thanked the Creator for the day, and hoped it would be a better one.

On the fifth day in Missouri it was very hot again. We were hassle free most of the day, and we were getting out to the countryside where there were less people. We were glad to be out where we were, with no stoplights, and free to walk non-stop. We were all in better spirits. We were only walking 21 miles today and that made it easier, too. Halfway through the day, Dennis pulled up in a support vehicle that picked him up at the airport, and everybody started cheering. The walk stopped for about 15 minutes, and we all got reacquainted.

Then he grabbed one of the Staffs and said he had to walk off some of the calories he picked up in D.C. He said that the people really fed him well. I said hey, everybody is going to have to go on a diet because we are eating so well. With the food donations, people were eating better on the walk than they were at home. I ate as much as I could everyday, because I knew I would burn those calories off. I didn't care about calories or fat. I pretty much ate anything I wanted. I stayed at 170 pounds throughout the walk, as opposed to my regular 180 to 190 lbs. It was good to know I didn't have to watch my calories.

After the remarks about how good we were eating on the walk,   Dennis told us everything was good in D.C. He said we would get plenty of coverage and various celebrities would be there. CNN news would be there, and Turner Broadcasting would be filming our walk for a documentary.   Kris Kristofferson would be there, having a concert for us, and an all Indian rock band named Redbone would be performing.

After the break, we got back into walking. Dennis asked me how it went while he was gone. I told him fine, until we got into the park. I told him about the Park Ranger's pulling their guns on me. He said I did the right thing by not letting it get out of hand. We shook hands and started walking even faster.

Dennis suggested we get some hand drums from the support vehicle, and we put two people up front singing songs. I remember when we passed through this one little town people were looking through their curtains at us, and some people got off their porches and went inside. I told him it seemed like they were worried we wanted to take the town back or something. Dennis said he heard the KKK operated in the area and that we didn't want to stop in any of these little towns. I didn't want any trouble, so I just prayed to the Creator to keep us all safe and sound. With the drumming going on it made the day seem to go a little faster.

While we were walking side by side I told Dennis that I was looking forward to the Sundance coming up in a couple of months. He asked me if I was walking and fasting now and then. I told him I had done it twice and I would do it again tomorrow. He said, "At the Sundance you learn to appreciate water." He said water sustains life and if everyone were to Sundance they would really learn to appreciate the gift of water. I took out my canteen and, even though the water was warm, I took a good long drink and thanked the Creator for giving us this water. As Indians, we are the caretakers of Mother Earth and we want everyone to respect the water and everything else that Creator and Mother Earth have given us. I'm a traditional Indian and I don't take anything for granted. I thank the Creator for what we have. We need to keep the Earth clean for future generations, but some people think, "I won't be here, so who cares?" The Indians call this planet Mother Earth because this **is** our Mother, and you wouldn't throw dirt on your Mother, or gasoline on your Mother, or pollution on your Mother.

As we crossed the USA, we made sure we didn't throw any garbage on the road, and we always left our campsite clean. One time I saw someone stomp out his cigarette, and I asked him if he would put a cigarette out on his Mother. He said I was right and picked up the butt and put it in his pocket. As I crossed the country, I would see more and more dirt the closer we got to the cities. I told one of the walkers I wished we could just pick up all the dirt. He said "Where would we put it, in a landfill?" I said the whole planet was going to wind up being one giant landfill if we didn't start taking care of the plastic, and the garbage, and the nuclear waste. I was beginning to feel that the only safe place to live was on a reservation.

My reservation in Oneida, Wisconsin is in real good shape because of the money they get from our two casinos. Some other Indian tribes aren't as fortunate if they don't have gambling or some other means of outside money. On some reservations, big nuclear waste companies are aware of how poor the reservations are, and they try to get the Indian people to sell areas of land so they can dispose of their waste material. Knowing the Indians are poor, they try to pay them off. The Oneida's don't have that problem because of the gambling revenue. Some Indians aren't as lucky, and these companies try to dump the waste on their reservations. This is one of our issues on the walk, and we will be bringing it up in D.C. Ninety percent of the Indians we spoke to coming across the U.S don't want the waste either. So, they had better leave the tribes alone and find some place else to put it.

Carter Camp has been an Indian activist for the past 23 years. The main reason he joined us on the Walk and represented the Ponca Tribe in Oklahoma was so he could speak out about this big company offering them several million dollars to put waste on their land. He wants to let people know how they keep trying to put these dumpsites on their reservation. Also, he walked for Leonard Peltier's freedom. Everyone on the walk had their own reasons for being there, and we often talked about the different grievances we wanted to talk about in D.C. We were all looking forward to airing these grievances when we got there.

We had to walk through Missouri for 12 days, and that was a little long to be in that state, but we took our time because we only had to go 266 miles. All in all, our stay in Missouri wasn't that bad, but with our problem with the park rangers and the people yelling things at us, it wasn't that good either. We only had one more day to go, and then our next state would be Illinois. On our last night in Missouri, we were put up in a gymnasium and had real good food. Dennis spoke about the Walk for Justice, and some local Indians invited us to a Sweat Lodge. We always liked to get together, rest our bodies, say our prayers, and let the Creator hear us.

Even though I talked about the Sweat Lodge before, I will take some time to tell you more about it now. It's the sacred Stone People's Lodge. Also known as the Sweat Lodge. It is very sacred to the Indian people. It's used to cleanse the body, mind, and soul. Through sweat and prayer, we clean our bodies of toxins and our minds of negativity, and heighten our spirits to come into the right relationship with ourselves, everything that surrounds us, Mother Earth, and the Creator. Because it is an ancient, spiritual ceremony, we hold it very sacred. It is our church. We go there to sing and pray to the Creator.

The lodge is made of willow branches. It's shaped like an Igloo and covered with blankets to shut out all light. The mound of dirt outside is the altar. It is sacred and powerful. Once the ceremony begins, we do not cross the front of the lodge, the altar, or the fire pit. The fire pit is where all the rocks are heated by a very hot fire. It is kept hot by the fire keepers. They wash the stones, lay the stones in the correct location, sage and cedar the stones, and get the stones as hot as they possibly can before they are brought into the lodge. This is where the heat in a Sweat Lodge comes from. The first four stones are put in the four direction signs...south, north, east, and west. The Lodge Keeper, the person running the lodge, makes sure that the stones are put in this formation. The bigger the pit and the bigger the Sweat Lodge, the more rocks you have, and the more people you have. Also, the hotter it will be. It's totally dark inside the lodge. Once the flap is closed, you can't see your hands in front of you. Once the rocks come in, the only light in there is the glow of the hot stones. You can barely see the other individuals' faces.

When the rocks are at their hottest point, the leader will signal that the ceremony is ready to begin.

People enter the Lodge on their hands and knees, to humble themselves to the Creator. As you pass through the door, you say "Mitakuye Oyasin" or "All my relations" and move clock-wise into the Lodge, surrounding the pit. At the end, everyone will be sitting shoulder to shoulder facing the rocks in the pit. You wait for the Lodge Keeper to bring in the four directional rocks, and the last thing to come into the Lodge before they close the flap is a bucket of water. The Lodge Keeper will be throwing this water onto the rocks throughout the praying and throughout the ceremony. It could last an hour, or, depending on the Lodge Keeper, it could go on for several hours. They usually go on for four rounds, which means throwing the water on the rocks four different times for the four directions, but they can go as long as the Lodge Keeper wants it to go.

Each individual says a prayer. You can pray out loud, or to yourself. Each person has to wait to say their prayer, so there's no way to tell how long the sweat will take. The last thing to come into the Sweat Lodge, after all four rounds have been completed, is the Chanupa—the Sacred Pipe. After everyone has smoked the sacred Chanupa the sweat is over, and everyone exits the lodge the same way they came in—on their hands and knees to humble themselves before the Creator, Mother Earth, and all your relations. If it gets too hot for an individual, you can leave, and you should not be embarrassed. It is not a contest of survival. You are there to pray for yourself and your brothers and sisters-all your relations.

What most people fail to remember, though, is that we are **all** related. You pray for Mother Earth and your loved ones. This can be a very powerful healing ceremony. Many individuals go on a fast before a Sweat Lodge ceremony. This can heighten your awareness. If it gets too hot for **me**, I put my face to the cool, cool earth. When you are offered water to drink, remember that this is the lifeblood of Mother Earth. You can feel the healing energy flowing through you. If you don't want to drink the water you can pour it on the rocks.

One custom of the Sweat Lodge is making prayer ties for private needs, or healing for your family. You use the colors black, yellow, white, red, green, and blue. Green is for Mother Earth, Blue for Father Sky, and the rest are the colors of the four directions, the colors of the people on Mother Earth. You make prayer ties by putting sacred tobacco into little bundles. As you make the little ties you pray, then you tie them off. You carry them into the Sweat Lodge with you and hang them over the rafters of the lodge so that when you throw water and sage over the rocks, the steam will go through the prayer ties and carry your prayers to the Creator. You're not obligated to do it, but if you want to, you can.

Indians believe that when you are in that dark Sweat Lodge and you don't have any clothes on, it is like being back in your Mother's womb. It is customary to offer a gift to the medicine person or Lodge Keeper for their special work and prayers, usually items like blankets, tobacco, special rocks, feathers, or sage. After all this, there is usually a potluck dinner—a feast for all the people of the Sweat Lodge, the people who helped, the Fire Keepers, and the Lodge Keeper. This feast could go on for a few hours. Everyone brings a dish and they sit around and talk about the sweat and other things. It is a very spiritual experience. Anytime I hear of a sweat, I go out of my way to be there, because they keep me strong, and give me a chance to give thanks to the Creator. If you're ever invited to the Sweat Lodge, I urge you to seek it out and experience it for yourself. It affects everyone differently, and it is very religious to the Indian people.

The 26th of May was our last day in Missouri. We had a good sweat the night before, and everyone woke up recharged. After the morning circle we got on the road. We would be entering Illinois on May 27th, and would only have to walk 170 miles to get across that state. On our last day in Missouri a lot of people stopped and signed the petitions. A few miles before the Illinois border we could see some news vans ahead. I told everyone to put on their happy faces because the media was waiting. They were from Carbondale, Illinois and drove up to see us. They asked to speak to us. I told them they could walk along side or they could wait until we got to our first campsite in Illinois. They said they would meet us and take some pictures of the group walking across the bridge over the Mississippi, into Illinois.

ILLINOIS

Eventually we did get to the border, which was halfway over the bridge, and the news media were there with their cameras on us as we walked over the state line. It was good to have the media there to welcome us in. Anytime we could get the word out, we were all for it. The news media interviewed me for about 20 minutes. They covered all the ins and outs of the walk, and they were going to get it into the Illinois Metro newspaper in the morning. They said they were going to help us get additional coverage from other news media. They started the circle without me, because people wanted to get off their feet.

After the interview, I fell into the circle and it was the usual shoptalk. We always wanted to know where the stores were, what areas we should avoid, and what would be going on that night. With that, I made a mad dash for the telephone and told my wife we were now in our eighth state. She told me my Brother Dale had called from Wisconsin and said that he and a close friend of mine named Forest Okamash were going to meet us at the closest point of Wisconsin and Illinois 50 and walk with us. They would be coming up with a van full of people, bringing food and money. My brother was pretty excited since we hadn't seen each other in over a year. I was looking forward to seeing family. It eased some of my homesickness knowing that some good friends were coming in to join the walk for two days. After I hung up, I went to the nearest Burger King in the little town and had a nice meal. I went back to camp and wrote a letter and relaxed. Not soon after that, I blew out my lantern and went to sleep.

The next morning we had breakfast and the morning circle. We were all in a good mood knowing we were in Illinois. We all shook hands and Dennis told us we would only be walking 17 miles today, due to the fact it was one of the shortest states we would be walking through. I was looking forward to seeing my brother at about the halfway point through Illinois.

We walked for about an hour. We were going through a little town and I was looking for a paper box to see if I could find the article on the Walk for Justice. Sure enough, I saw one and we were smack dab on the front page with the headline "Native Americans Pause in Area During Cross Country Rights March". I was on the front page holding the eagle Staff. I bought several copies and told a guy to pass them out. During the lunch break we read what they had to say. It was a good article—very informative. Nothing out of the way happened that day. It was just an average day.

Another newspaper came out to interview us at the end of the day. They were from the Southern Illinois Sunday Paper. They heard about us from the Illinois Metro. They weren't really up on what we were walking about, so I told them about Leonard Peltier, and the other 15 reasons we were walking.

I'd like to tell you a little bit more about Leonard Peltier. He was born in 1944 at Grand Forks, North Dakota and he is from the Ojibwa Tribe. He had a difficult childhood, moving with his family from copper mines to logging camps. When his parents separated he was placed in an Indian School in North Dakota where he encountered strict discipline. He returned to live with his mother, but at the age of 14 he left home to find work. At the age of 20 he was part owner of an auto body shop in Seattle, Washington. I know him personally, and he is a very good person. I met him in 1972 and he had been an active A.I.M. member since 1970. Leonard Peltier participated in many A.I.M. activities including the B.I.A. takeover in 1972. In August of 1973, Peltier undertook the Sundance, a sacred vision-seeking ceremony practiced by many plains Indians. To endure pain to induce a vision, his chest was pierced with bone and he would dance before the sacred tree for four days without food or water. After the Sundance, Peltier returned to Seattle, but spent the next year and a half traveling the country. In the summer of 1975 he was living on the

Pine Ridge reservation in South Dakota. There are many conflicting reports regarding the events of June 26, 1975, which eventually led to Peltier's conviction and jail sentencing. This much is clear: FBI agents Jack Coler and Ronald Williams, and Pine Ridge resident Joe Killsright were killed in a shootout near Oglala, South Dakota on the Pine Ridge reservation. Leonard was among a group of Lakota engaged in a shooting exchange with the FBI Agents. The FBI and the Indian Police reinforcements soon arrived and returned fire, killing Killsright. Peltier and the others hid out with family and friends, then slipped into Canada, where he was arrested early in July, 1976.

In a controversial and disputed trial in Fargo, North Dakota, from which 80% of the defendants testimony was excluded, Peltier was convicted of murdering the two FBI Agents. He was sentenced to two consecutive life terms, and was transferred to a high security penitentiary at Marion, Illinois, after a brief transfer to a prison camp in California. In many foreign countries, Peltier is considered a political prisoner of the United States.

New evidence regarding the Pine Ridge shootout has been written by Peter Mathiesson's book, "In the Spirit of Crazy Horse," disputing Peltier's involvement in the murder of the FBI Agents. Peltier has maintained his innocence all along, and we know the circumstances surrounding the case. We are bound and determined to get him out of prison soon. It bears mentioning again - to find out more about Leonard's case, rent the movie called "Incident at Oglala," by

Robert Redford. It tells all the facts, and after you see it you too will ask why this man is in prison. That's why a lot of Indian people consider him to be a P.O.W.

After my interview with the newspaper reporter, I thanked him for his interest, and he said he would contact other people in the media in Illinois, and the upcoming states of Indiana and Ohio. He told me it would be in the next morning's paper. I went back to the camp and we all sat around chatting.

Dennis let me know that it would be getting hot going though the next states, and he asked me if I would go out in the morning to get the main distance out of the way. I would be walking in the cool of the morning, and also less traffic. Then they would drive everybody else out in the support vehicles after breakfast and finish the rest of the walk with me. I told him I would welcome the time alone. He told Dave Patton to get an old fashioned alarm clock so I could get up early, whenever I wanted to. Dave, his wife and son, and I got even closer. We needed a yellow safety light to put on top of the cab of the vehicle. In addition, he would put his flashing lights on, and there would also be a Dayglo banner, which said "Walker Ahead". With all the new equipment, I figured it would be safe to walk at night.

Dennis said some people might be angry because I could really cover some miles. He told me not to worry about it, because it saved them from walking all day in the sun and sometimes would even give them an extra day off. I decided to bring a pair of running shoes so I could walk part of the way and I could run part of the way. This was done for safety purposes, too, one person walking at night with a safety vehicle. All the roads coming up were very narrow and it would be safer for one person.

The next morning, Dave got me up at 1:30 am and we took off at 2:00 am. It was a good thing we had all the safety features, because even at night, trucks and cars came barreling by. If he saw someone coming up behind us, he would honk his horn twice to let me know it was time to move over and get out of the way. Dave and his family were very good at making sure I had the proper food and water. I have to thank them for taking real good care of me.

It was kind of a foggy, misty morning, and around 3:00 am I saw movement in the grass. I didn't know if it was a dog, or a cat, or a raccoon. Suddenly in the glow of the support vehicle's lights I saw a possum, and his eyes were really red from the lights. He looked at me like, "What the hell are you doing out here at this time of the night?" He walked with me for almost 10 minutes, and I found it amazing how tame he was and how he was staying right with me. Then he cocked his head and looked at me as if to say, "Enjoy your walk", and he went off into the brush. I became kind of fond of that possum. I would think about him from time to time and have a good laugh. I wish I had caught it on videotape.

It felt good to walk in the cool of the night. It was a whole different ballgame. It showed me that nature is pretty smart, staying out of the heat. I saw all kinds of nocturnal creatures, like owls and bats. It was fun. I enjoyed the solitude. As I said, Dave stayed 100 to 200 yards behind me and I spent a lot of time lost in my own thoughts. It was almost like a meditation. Sometimes, I would walk as fast as I could. One time, Dave clocked me walking five miles in an hour. He did this without me knowing it and I was really surprised. Other walkers would come out to walk with me in the morning sometimes, and I would tell them I really needed to cover miles, and if they couldn't keep up, then they would need someone to follow in another vehicle because Dave didn't have any room. As I said, sometimes I would try to do the whole mileage, whether it was 18 or 24 miles, or whatever.

On the first day of walking by myself in Illinois I walked for five hours. I got to see the sun come up and experience the fresh morning air. When I would look back and see the Winnebago camper pulling up I was almost sorry to see them, because I knew I would be hearing complaints about walking too fast. But, it was nothing serious. Everyone had their own reasons for walking.

The Oneida Indians had somewhat of a reputation for walking long distances. I felt like these genes were passed on to me because I loved the walking. I really don't like running, but I love to walk. I must admit, there were days when my feet were really hurting and I didn't want to walk. I said to myself, the first things I'm going to do when I get back to Vegas, I'm going to kiss my wife and then kiss my car. On other days, I would think, I'm not going to use my car as much when I get home. But, the Eagle Staff I was carrying is what gave me power. Power beyond belief. I thanked the Creator for guiding me and the rest of the walkers through all those miles. I knew I would be thanking him at the Sundance in August. When I walked with the Staff I was always praying for Leonard and his release, and the well being of the other walkers. The praying helped me to deal with the homesickness and the sore feet. Believe me, there were days when I did have a hard time going on. But, the praying helped me. The Walk for Justice was as much a spiritual walk as it was a walk to bring attention to Leonard Peltier's case. When I look back, it was the best thing I ever did for myself, and for Leonard Peltier. I wouldn't trade the experience for anything.

We were all in good spirits, and now that we were in Illinois, we only had five more states to go. Also, I knew my brother Dale and my best friend Forest would be linking up with us out of Milwaukee. I knew that they and my whole family were following this walk across the United States. Dale and Forest would be meeting up with us in Salem, Illinois and that was just a couple of days away. This put extra pep in my step.

The second day of walking through Illinois was a 25-mile day. So far, people had been really friendly, but there were rumors circulating that when we got over to Indiana and Ohio the Ku Klux Klan had heard about us, and we would be walking right through their area. Dennis and I wondered if there would be any racial problems. We agreed to be more careful when we went through these areas.

On our third day in Illinois a couple named Craig and Jennifer Olsen put us up on their 10-acre farm during a three-day scheduled rest. This was very convenient because it was close to the main town. They also cooked for us the whole time. We really looked forward to these two and three-day rests, and the people always took really good care of us. I always looked for the nearest phone to make my phone calls, and then I would just go on R & R until it was time to walk again.

After our three-day rest we still had another five-day walk before we got to our next state. Before we left, we had a prayer ceremony and thanked the Olsens for taking such good care of us. Now we were on our way to Salem and I was looking forward to hooking up with my brother and other friends. I was in a really good mood that day. We had to walk 25 miles, and a lot of people drove by and gave us food and money donations. They told us they believed in what we were doing, and they wanted to sign our petition. We even had Sheriffs pull up and tell us it was a bad deal that Peltier got, and **they** signed our petition. We knew that what we were doing was right, but it was good reinforcement when law enforcement and city officials were signing our petition and telling us they were going to contact their congressmen. A lot of churches put us up along the way and we really appreciated it. Without them, there would have been a lot of nights spent in the cold, without any comfortable shelter.

On this particular day we were 18 miles into our walk when a car pulled up and a man told us he was a Pastor from the next town, which was Olney, and they wanted to put us up. They wanted to know how many of us there were so they could prepare a meal for everyone. I told him there were about 50 people and it would be approximately three hours before we got to town. The pastor's name was Reverend Jensen, and I shook his hand and thanked him for his support. We never went hungry anytime after we left San Francisco, and it was good people like this that made it possible. All along the way people from various towns would help us out. A lot of the people took walkers into their houses. Sometimes we would be there for two or three days.

As we were walking, I realized it was already the end of May, and I wondered where the time went. It seemed like only yesterday we were in the Rocky Mountains freezing our butts off, and now here we were, near the June weather of Illinois. This was only giving us one more month to get through the neighboring states of Indiana, Ohio, Virginia and West Virginia, then a short walk into D.C. We were looking forward to getting through Illinois, which was one of our shortest states, at only 170 miles.

We passed through a lot of small towns on the walk, and sometimes we wouldn't see a Burger King or McDonald's for several days. When we got near a town and I could smell a Burger King, I knew where I was heading. I just loved my junk food, and I didn't worry about eating it because I didn't have to worry about putting on the weight.

When we arrived in Olney, the people had everything set up for us. We were looking forward to setting up in the church basement because it was raining. We had a closing prayer and thanked the Creator for getting us through the day.

The next morning we prayed, saged off, and began to walk the 22 miles for the day. Throughout Illinois, I realized I was feeling more and more spiritual each step I took. I could only thank the Creator for making it possible for me to continue to be strong and make this walk. I was looking forward to seeing my brother. We would have a three-day break soon, and I felt compelled to ride back to Milwaukee to see my Mom, who I hadn't seen in over a year and a half. I knew in my heart it would be too hard to get back to the walk, so I decided to stay in Illinois and enjoy the time with my brother and my best friend.

The next day we got into Lawrenceville and we set up camp in a farmer's field. Tomorrow we had 23 miles to walk. That night, I was in my tent sleeping when I heard someone say "Wake up Harry Kindness". I heard my brother Dale and Forest. I got out of my tent and put a flashlight on them, and they came over and we embraced each other. I asked how the family was doing. They said everyone was fine and sent their best wishes. We sat up till the wee hours of the morning, even though we had to walk 23 miles as the last leg of Illinois. I didn't mind because I was so happy to see these guys.

In the morning Dennis told us we would be getting out of the state of Illinois today and going into Indiana. We set out and we had the whole day to talk and enjoy being together. I slowed down a bit, but the day went by really fast. The three days were just great.

When they left for Wisconsin, it was hard to see them leave. It was hard for them, too. They wanted to finish the rest of the walk into D.C., but couldn't do it because they had everyday, typical jobs, and they could have been replaced if they didn't go back to work. Dale reassured me he would be there when we walked into D.C. With that they left and I watched their car go over the hill and out of sight.

That day we would only be walking 11 miles before entering the state of Indiana at Vincennes. It was a good feeling to know we were only four states from our destination. Everyone else felt the same way and we couldn't walk fast enough. We would have to cover 191 miles to get through Indiana, and that meant walking through nine little towns. We would be covering 25 to 30 miles a day, except for the 11-mile day. This wasn't bad considering we had to cover 35 miles a day in some states. Mentally and physically it was getting easier and we were getting closer.

INDIANA

It was now June 4th, 1994, and in another 10 days we would be on the road for a full four months. Some days it seemed like we had been gone a year, and at other times it seemed like just a matter of weeks. It was just my mind playing tricks on me. Even though we had two, three, and four-day rests, with our longest rest being 10 days, sometimes it just seemed like this was an endless pilgrimage. It gave me a lot of time to think about our Indian ancestors who had to do forced marches, back in the 1800's. They couldn't stop at Burger King, or McDonald's, or 7-Eleven. Even though we didn't have a lot of the modern conveniences on our walk, imagine how hard it must have been back then.

We always saged off at the start of the day and at the end of day, and we made it a point to start the day with a prayer and end the day with a prayer. We always kept the Indian religion close to us, because we knew praying to the Creator brought everyone close together. It changed my whole way of thinking. I felt a lot closer to the Creator than I had in years, going to sweats and listening to people sing drum songs. I wouldn't trade it for anything. I can't express how it brought me back full circle.

I was only two and a half months from the Sundance, and all this praying and getting back on the red road was helping to strengthen my commitment for the spiritual aspect of dancing. I had gotten off that path before the Walk for Justice, but as long as I was carrying that Staff, in my mind I was praying. And that was **preparing** me for the Sundance. This would be the next major highlight in my life. I had my eagle bone whistle since the second month on the walk. Whenever I had a private moment, I would take out the whistle and hold onto it. I was really happy to have it in my possession.

During the walk, I came into contact with three other Indian brothers who were Sundancers, and they had filled me in on what I could expect. Dennis was a full- fledged Sundancer and he helped a lot, telling me how to prepare myself for going without food and water for four days, and dancing from sunup till sundown. I would be lying if I said I wasn't scared, but I knew in my heart that I would be prepared. This was something I had to do, not for myself, but for my people, and for the sickness in my family. I was willing to make whatever sacrifice I had to make. The

Sundance never left my mind during the whole walk. I would only have one month to rest up before the Sundance ceremony in Pipestone, Minnesota, but I knew I would get well rested back in Las Vegas, after the walk.

After our first day we would be going to Vincennes, Indiana for a two-day rest. The news media met with us, and we informed them about Leonard Peltier's case. They were mainly interested in covering the walk in respect to his case. They let the rest of the media in the adjacent towns know about us, and they, too, were interested in interviewing us. At the end of our designated 25 miles, Dennis Banks had a circle, and we all said a prayer. Dennis brought to our attention that Leonard Peltier, as he had throughout the walk, was sending faxes out to us, through his attorney, expressing his thanks and gratitude. On this particular day he was thanking everyone for getting this far, and he was glad we had made it to Indiana. He had been reading in the paper about our accomplishments over the months and he was really proud of us.

Most of the walkers didn't know Leonard, like I did. But everyone was really moved by his letters, faxes, and effort to make contact with us. It really kept the walkers going. Dennis would stay in touch by phone on a week to week basis, keeping Leonard informed on our progress. Obviously, Leonard was very interested in us putting the spotlight back on his case. He was well aware of what we had been doing over the months and he gave us his whole-hearted support. People from all over the world have supported Leonard Peltier, and the news of this walk was in newspapers as far away as Thailand.

Over the months I had been sending all my news clippings back to Las Vegas. I wanted to put together a real good portfolio, from start to finish, for the Walk for Justice. It was kind of painstaking to make sure I got all the articles, but it was worth it. When I return to Vegas I can look back on what happened from time to time, and have a pretty good picture.

We got into Vincennes, and I quickly went to the nearest phone, called my wife, and told her to send me a care package. I wanted to know how things were in Sin City, good old Las Vegas, Nevada. I also needed a new tent after four months on the road, camping in all kinds of weather. I told Karen to go to the nearest camping store and get one out to me quick. After walking a long day, or part of the night, I hated sleeping in a damp, musty tent. I filled her in on where we were, and she assured me she would have a new house sent out to me by FedEx.

This was the 6th of June, and Dennis Banks brought to my attention that there was a pow wow in a neighboring town. We needed to go there and seek their help, because two of our support vehicles had finally run into mechanical problems. Dennis suggested that we go to the pow wow and ask them to have a blanket dance for us.

Four walkers and myself went into the town, which was named Pleasantville, where they were having the pow wow. We asked if we could come into the arena with our drums and play five songs or so, and have a blanket dance so we could raise some money to fix our vehicles. During a blanket dance you take a blanket out to the middle of the powwow grounds, and the person on the PA system asks for help from people in the audience. He asks them to give a little or a lot, and while we drum and sing a song, anyone who wants to help will dance out to the blanket and contribute money. After they explained that we were the Walk for Justice, people came out non-stop. When the blanket dance was over and we counted all the money, we had over $800.00. Considering the number of people that were there, $800.00 was a lot of money.

When we returned to the campsite we went to Dennis's trailer and told him how much we had. We turned the money over to the Treasurer. Next morning circle Dennis let everyone know that we had gotten the $800.00 to fix our vehicles so they could carry our luggage and supplies for the rest of the walk. Dennis also told us that there was a whole school of masseuses that was coming into camp on our day off, and they were going to give free massages all day long.

Whenever we got into one of these little towns and had a day off it was great to get a little duded up and go into town, get something to eat, and maybe take in a movie. I almost felt like a gypsy because I was always some place different.

It would take us nine days to get through the state of Indiana, and the people there were very good to us. But, as always, we were looking forward to getting into our next state.

Indiana - wonder where they came up with that name!

OHIO

I got up at 2:00 am on our last day in Indiana, anxious to get going. As usual, Dave Patton and his family followed close behind. It was a very cool morning, and I was looking forward to the walk. I walked at a real fast pace. During a 15-minute break I sat on the side of the highway and thought about how the walk would be over soon, and about all of the miles we had covered. So when Dave told me we only had about 11 miles to go before we crossed the bridge into Ohio it just seemed like a stroll through the mall.

We finished the break, and got back on good old 50 for the last few miles of Indiana. It didn't seem like it took any time at all before I saw a frame type bridge, and the sign welcoming us to Ohio. As I crossed the bridge I saw a police car with its lights on, and I wondered what was going on. When I got up to him, he said, "You're the guys who have been walking across the United States for the last five months". He shook my hand and said "I got to hand it to you". When I got over the hill there was a bunch of people waiting for me, and they welcomed me into Ohio. They wanted to sign the petition, so I directed them to the support vehicle. It was the 13th of June. We would be going through nine towns and cover a total of 150 miles before we got into Virginia. Once we got through Ohio we would only have two states to go before we got to D.C., and that was really a good feeling.

Dennis Banks had made plans to have a big rally in Cincinnati. At the rally we would have some high profile news media, and we were welcoming all the attention we could get. When we made camp that first night in Ohio, Dennis told me there would be a meeting the next morning to prepare all the walkers for the march. The march would be held during lunch hour, right smack dab in the middle of downtown Cincinnati, so people could see A.I.M. on the Walk for Justice. We would be beating our drums and singing traditional Native American songs. We also had Indians and non-Indians from the Cincinnati area joining in, and expected to have about 300 people, all told. We had heard the Ku Klux Klan was going to harass us going through Ohio, but we didn't worry about it. We had heard rumors in other states, too, but nothing ever came of it. We were going to be taking a lunch break at the church in downtown Cincinnati where we were going to have the rally. We were going to get there around 11:00, and various people would join us then. This was the most populated area we had walked through. We went through the downtown area because we were getting closer to D.C. and we wanted to make as many people aware of our Walk as we could.

When we got to the church everyone found a place to sit on the floor, and we had a crowd of about 300. After lunch, people of all races-black, white, Indian, Asian-got together for the walk to the rally site. We were carrying the Staffs, the Indian Flag, and banners and signs with various slogans. Dennis held a pre-rally meeting and told us to obey all the traffic rules. We would be walking on the sidewalk and not in the street. The drummers would be behind Dale VanFleet and myself. After we got the "dos and don'ts" we lined up on the sidewalk and began a one-mile march to the downtown area. It was a strong feeling to see all this unity from people we didn't even know. As we marched I could see various people slowing down and wondering what the hell was going on. We had all the Indians in the front, and the people from other races behind us. It was this way only because it was an A.I.M. event. It was a great way to get attention. You can see people of all races on a street, people from any foreign country, and most people think nothing of it. But when American Indians get together, **American** Indians, people who were here before anyone else came, it gets attention. We are a curiosity. We draw attention. People would ask us what was going on, and we would tell them that

163

we were the Walk for Justice. When they asked about the petition I would send them to the people who could help them out. Although it was a parade-like atmosphere, we were still serious about what we were doing. I could see people peeking from behind curtains, people looking down from the upper floors, and secretaries getting up from their desks to look at us. It looked like they were going to start circling the wagons at any minute.

When we got to the rally there were already people there as part of our group. All kinds of business people were having their lunches in the square, and Dennis got up on a platform that was set up with a PA system. I stood on the stage with the Staff, and another guy was on the other side of Dennis with a Leonard Peltier banner. There was a lot of local news media present, and Dennis let them know what the walk was all about. Dennis spoke in depth to the crowd of 400 to 500 people. I talked about the Peltier case and why we were walking. After about an hour, the crowd responded with a standing ovation. When the rally was over, everyone had a second lunch in the shops located throughout the plaza. It was a good rally and reached a lot of people.

That night, we stayed at the church where we first stopped. I went to a phone and called my wife to tell her we were in Ohio. She let me know that she had sent out my new tent and a care package. Man, did I look forward to getting that! She also told me that my brother would be in Washington, D.C. when I got there. He had gotten some time off work, and he could stay for a couple of days. He was really glad that he was able to join me on the Walk earlier.

We had about one month left on the Walk, and 148 more miles to go through the state of Ohio, with one two-day rest period. We were going to get through Ohio pretty fast. We were told that we would have some good rest days when we got to West Virginia. It was good to know that I would be back in Las Vegas with my wife and friends in about a month, and that the Sundance was just a couple of months away. I was really in high spirits at this point, but I sure did miss my wife.

I went back to the church parking lot and picked through the gear until I found my backpack and sleeping bag. It felt like I was at rummage sale. I found myself a real nice cozy sleeping spot under a big, old, oak table. Throughout the trip, I always managed to find a spot under a table when we were at a church, a gym, or at a college. I had somewhat of a reputation of being a gopher because I always slept under something. I set up my spot, and then we had a big dinner, where people from neighboring communities brought food. Dennis talked about Leonard and the Walk. We sang songs, and a lot of people expressed an interest in Indian culture. Dennis introduced me as the main Staff carrier and told about some of the things I had gone through, especially my trip over Monarch Pass in the blizzard.

I always look up to Dennis. He is from the old school. He had done a lot for the Indian people and I always admired him for that. He was my hero, and I kind of put him high up on a pedestal. He is truly one of a kind.

The gathering went on until around 11:00 that night. Dennis got on the PA system and told us that we had a long walk the next day, so everyone said their good-byes. With that, somebody yelled, "Lights out!" I went to sleep and got ready for another day on that Red Road.

I got up in the wee hours of the morning and started my usual routine. I got into my gear real quietly, and I knew that in about five hours people would be getting that rude awakening from Rooster. I hadn't heard the Rooster crow for at least two months, and to tell the truth, I kind of missed it. I looked around at people curled up in their sleeping bags and I felt kind of jealous. But, I knew I had to get out on the road, so I crept out the back exit door where Dave and his family were waiting. We started walking the 25 miles for the day.

Down the road a ways, I took a little break and called my wife to wish her good morning. Being away from her for this long put an ache in my heart that wouldn't go away. I sure appreciated what she was doing to support us so I could do what I needed to do. I just wanted to tell her how much I loved her, and missed her and that I couldn't even "be" without her.

Later in the day, people pulled up and asked to sign the petition. They had seen the news coverage of the rally. A lot of people also gave us donations. Since I was usually the first one out, I would generally run into people and the news media.

While in Ohio we would be taking an extended rest at a historical site where the Indian Warrior, Tecumseh, used to speak before going out on his raids. It was in a cave, and he would get up to 2000 people in there. Everyone could hear him because of the acoustics. I was looking forward to seeing the cave. We would also be speaking at the University of Ohio, and people were looking forward to that because the more media that came out, the more coverage we got.

The rest of the walkers caught up with me at about 8:00 in the morning. At the end of the day a farmer gave us several acres of his land to set up our gear. There was also going to be a sweat, and everyone was really looking forward to that because it had been about three weeks since the last one. The farmer's name was Chuck. He was a horse breeder, and he had heard about us on the news. It was a beautiful farm and he let us stay on his land.

After we set up the mailman arrived with a big package for me. It was my tent and various other items I was looking forward to. I was glad that Karen had sent a two-man tent, because now I could get my backpack in there with me too. Getting a package from home made me feel some comfort on the road. A part of Karen was with me for a while. I'd think of how she packed the "care package" for me, and know she sent it with her love.

There was a Sweat Lodge built on the property that had been erected by some Indians, and Dennis told us we would be running a sweat all night. It would hold about 12 people, so we would keep going until everyone that wanted to had gone in. It was really hot. It was like having a non-stop massage on my feet. After the sweat I was totally relaxed, and I went back to my new two-man tent and fell fast asleep.

The next day was a rest day, and we would be going over to the University. They were going to have a meal for us, and Dennis was going to speak in the auditorium about the Walk for Justice. We would be selling T-shirts and crafts that we had made, and we would use the money for food, gas, and car repairs. We had done this on the whole trip, so this was nothing new.

Dennis spoke for about an hour and a half and filled everyone in on the details of Peltier's case and what we would be doing in D.C. Afterwards, there was a question and answer period that went on for over an hour. After Dennis finished speaking, I was invited to appear on the campus radio station for an hour interview. Once again, I filled them in on all the details.

That night, the Dean of the campus came to us and said we were more than welcome to use two dorms that were available because some people had gone home for spring break. We were welcome to take showers, and he said they would leave the cafeteria open for 24 hours. Dennis decided that we would stay at the campus for three days because we had access to phones and televisions. So, we would walk everyday and then shuttle back to the campus.

This was an extra treat, and that's what we did. The University also gave us a $500.00 donation.

The 25 miles we walked every day didn't seem like much until we got on that shuttle and went back to the campus. Then you would look at things you had seen and places you had been, and it seemed like a long way.

After three days on the campus I felt like a college boy, and I got to like it. We had phones and I was able to sleep in a soft bed. At the end of the three days we held a pipe ceremony, and everybody said prayers and saged off. They took care of us and we gave them some Indian culture back.

The next day we went to the cave where Tecumseh and his people met. We had an early morning pipe ceremony and sang a few Native drum songs. It was an eerie feeling being in the cave and on the spot where this great warrior had stood. I stood where all the Indian people had been when Tecumseh gave his speeches. I felt the power.

We spent about an hour there, and then went back to continue the walk. We headed for Coolville, Ohio, where some people were going to put us up on a dairy farm. The owners had heard my interview on the campus radio station, and they offered to put us up for as long as we needed. I knew the Creator was taking good care of us all along the way. Coolville would be the last town in Ohio, and then we would be going into West Virginia.

At the morning circle Dennis told us we would have three days of rest in West Virginia, and we would pass through five towns. The part of the state we were going through would only be about 190 miles. This made us all upbeat because it was a relatively short distance. We walked the last 22 miles in Ohio on the 27th of June, 1994. Coolville lived up to its name. Everything was real laid back and everything went real smooth. Cool!

WEST VIRGINIA

We left Ohio and got to Parkersburg, West Virginia on June 28th. The closer we got to D.C., the longer the days got. I spoke to my wife when we got into West Virginia and it was great to tell her I would be coming home next month. She told me she would have to celebrate the Fourth of July by herself. I told her I would give her a call on the Fourth, and I would see her in less than a month.

I had lost 20 pounds and gone through three pairs of shoes on the walk, and I didn't know what I was going to do with my shoes when I was finished. Did I want to throw them away, get them resoled, have them bronzed, or just keep them as a memento of the Walk for Justice?

I was really on a high knowing we only had West Virginia and Virginia to go. I hadn't gotten sick, and I knew that the Creator had been taking care of me. A lot of people had shared their water bottles, and most everybody got sick at one time or another. I never shared my water and I never got a cold, or flu, or anything. I also took a vitamin C and a large quantity of odorless garlic capsules every day.

We had walked 21 miles to get to Parkersburg. Dennis let me know that the next two states would be the most dangerous up to this point, because the road was really narrow and these states were almost as hilly as Colorado. Also, a lot of the roads didn't have any white lines. This meant I would have to cover more miles at night, by myself, so we could keep from putting too many people on the road at one time. We decided that I should get as many solo miles under my hat as I could. We were close to D.C. and we didn't want any mishaps at this point.

We would go through 10 towns, and we would cover 192 miles on Highway 50 while passing through West Virginia. We would walk anywhere from 18 to 25 miles a day. We were able to slow the pace down over these last few states. We had walked so fast through the other states that we would have some time to rest a little before we got to Washington D.C.

The last time I had been in West Virginia was in 1972 when myself and another Indian activist came through the state on our way to the B.I.A. takeover. I had not been back this way in more than 20 years, and I wondered if it was going to be anything like it was then. Would there be any violence, would anything get out of hand, or would it just be a peaceful walk? We wanted peace. Twenty years ago A.I.M. was a radical and sometimes violent group.

We would be stopping at a campus in West Virginia, and they already had us booked into national parks. The parks were very clean, and they took very good care of us. We had showers and it was great. I enjoyed the state very much, and the scenery was incredible. The one thing that sticks out in my mind is something that happened early one morning.

Halfway through West Virginia I was still getting up early to cover the majority of the miles for the day. The roads in the state were blacker than black, and although I had a flashlight, I never turned it on while I was walking. On this particular morning, Dave Patton rolled up along side and told me we had just passed a convenience store, and since we were heading into desolate country he asked me if I would be alright while he went back, fueled up, and got some coffee.

I told him I had no problem walking in the dark. He told me he would be back in 15 or 20 minutes. I was just walking with the Staff, thinking how far we had gone, and how peaceful it was. Nothing had ever come my way while walking in the dark, but on this particular morning I happened to hear a crunching sound and movement in the woods. I didn't think much of it because I had seen all kinds of animals on the walk, including wolves, deer, and mountain goats. I really wasn't surprised to hear movement. As I continued walking I could hear twigs and branches snapping, up off the ground, and I figured that whatever it was, was out there maybe 200 or 300 yards in the thick woods, in total darkness, and it was big. I took out my flashlight and I couldn't see anything, but I could still hear movement. I knew it was big, because the branches I heard snapping and breaking weren't little twigs. Since I was by myself I was concerned that it was a bear or something, and it would come out of the woods after me. It seemed to be following my movements, step for step. This went on for close to 10 minutes. I shined my light back in there, and this time I saw some **green eyes**. But the thing that made my hair stand up on the back of my neck was that, not only were the eyes green, but they were at least six feet or more off the ground! I wondered if this was a bear standing on its hind legs, or who knows what.

Most Native cultures talk about the Sasquatch, or Bigfoot, or any of the other names they have for the same big, hairy creature, and I was beginning to wonder if I was going to see one, up close and personal. In any case, I was starting to get really nervous. I thought to myself, if anything comes running out of there, the only weapon I have is this flashlight and the end of the Sacred Staff. No sooner had I thought this than I saw lights coming up behind me, and I sure hoped it was Dave Patton. I waved to him and he pulled up and asked me if I wanted some coffee. I told him what had been happening, so he turned the car around and turned the lights into the woods.   We heard something running back in, breaking tree limbs as it went. We knew that it must have been something big because there was too much noise for it to be a raccoon or something like that. It definitely got my heart pumping and my adrenaline flowing. That was one time I got a little nervous out there by myself. We never did figure out what it was, but I'll sure never forget those green eyes staring back at me from the dark woods.

We made it through three different towns, and it was the second of July. We were now in Grafton, West Virginia, where we were scheduled to have a two-day break to celebrate the Fourth of July. I gave myself a treat and broke out the plastic. I told my wife I was going to rent a motel, rest my feet in the Jacuzzi, and just sleep for two days. Also, I wanted to see a couple of movies and eat in some nice restaurants for a change.

I got a room at the Motorlodge Motel, and put a friend of mine, Bruce Johnston, in charge of all my camping gear. He asked me where I was staying and wanted to know if he could use my shower. I told him that that was a fair trade-off. Next thing I know, after **he** used my shower, my room wound up being a shower haven for more than half the walkers. I didn't mind, though, because I knew I had the room and the shower for two days, and I told everyone that anybody could use the shower or phone if they wanted to, but no one was going to stay, because I wanted my privacy and some time to relax. Some of the local people in the area invited many of the walkers into their houses and let them use their bathroom facilities. They had heard about the Walk for Justice and wanted to do anything they could to help us out.

We still had 85 miles to go before we would get through West Virginia, and I had heard that the next few days were going to be really rough on the feet because there was a lot of hilly, even mountainous terrain. So I used the two days over the Fourth of July to really rest up. Even though we were 90% of the way through the walk I wasn't going to take these last miles for granted. I had walked through all kinds of terrain, from flat as a pancake desert in Nevada, to the 11,312-foot elevation of Monarch Pass in Colorado, down to the winding and hilly roads of Missouri. I figured it couldn't be any worse. I was just going to take in the scenery and enjoy every mile of it.

On the Fourth of July, I celebrated the fact that we only had 10 more days left to walk, but somehow I just couldn't feel good about **our** independence on the Fourth of July, as long as Leonard Peltier was locked up. At this point, my adrenaline was really pumping and all I could think about was D.C., D.C. It was a natural high, and we were expecting a big turnout when we got there. In addition, the Sundance was only a month away. It was something I was looking forward to and I had wanted to accomplish for the past two years. I knew that when I finished the walk I would be ready for the Sundance. I knew I would complete the full circle when I stood at the Tree of Life and thanked the Creator for getting me across the country and to the Sundance, and prayed for my people.

On the Fourth I spent the day in bed watching TV. It was great to lay in bed with that remote, experiencing one of the creature comforts I had become accustomed to before the Walk. But it also made me think about some of the cold nights and the long, hot days we had spent on the walk, without any electronic conveniences. I knew we would be back on the road tomorrow morning and we would have to get the rest of the 192 miles out of the way. I called my wife and wished her a happy Fourth of July, and then I went to sleep.

The next morning Dave Patton and his family picked me up at 2:00 in the morning and we got back out on Highway 50. Dave brought me a McDonald's breakfast and we sat on the tailgate of the pick-up and caught up on the last couple of days. After our chat, we started out. It was going to be a 21-mile day. I walked for about three hours, and we took another break. We could take a few more breaks now, due to the fact that we didn't have to cover as many miles. We had already covered about 11 miles that day when the rest of the walkers caught up with us.

Everybody asked me how I liked my stay in the Motorlodge, and I told them it was great. Dennis told me I was getting spoiled and there wouldn't be any more of that motel stuff. He said the next he knew I would be getting shuttled back and forth to the Holiday Inn, and he started laughing. There was a rumor that when we got to Virginia a gathering would be set up for us to talk about the Leonard Peltier case at Virginia State University. Virginia was going to be the shortest state, other than Maryland, so it was going to be a breeze to get through. It took us four days to get through the rest of the counties and the country roads in West Virginia. It was almost heaven.

Country roads, take me to Virginia - one state closer to home.

VIRGINIA

We arrived at the Virginia State line on Friday, the Eighth of July, 1994. Everybody was in good spirits, knowing we only had one more state to finish, and 93 more miles to our final march into D.C.

We got into Winchester on the ninth. I called my wife and updated her on all the gossip, as I had been doing over the last five months. I told her where we were, what was going on, and what was **going** to be going on. We had a verbal celebration together. She was really happy it was almost over. My brother, she confirmed, would be flying in to meet me for three days in D.C.

It seemed appropriate to wear my traditional native regalia for the last mile, when I would be walking into D.C, proudly carrying the Staff. We planned to get into D.C. the night before, and then walk the final mile to the rally at Lafayette Park the next morning. I called Karen again and told her to send all my regalia to me. I told her I would get a motel the night we got into D.C., and she could overnight it to me there.

Dennis would also be wearing his traditional regalia, and everybody else would be wearing red T-shirts that said "Free Leonard Peltier - The Walk for Justice". All the walkers would be in formation behind us. We definitely wanted to have some color coordination and to let everyone know we meant business, and wanted to look our best. Some people in the group wore their traditional regalia, also.

After walking 25 miles into Virginia, we only had three more 25 mile-days, and then two rest days, where everyone would be getting ready for the final walk into D.C. So, the rest of the trip was going to be something like a casual stroll. We knew the Walk for Justice would be over in four days. We only had 50 miles to go before crossing over a bridge into D.C.

The 25-mile days went quickly, and we were closing in on our final destination. We set up in Glen Carlyn Park, which was 20 miles from D.C. This was a rallying point on a hill and we could see D.C. from where we were. It was a heart pumping experience. The next day was a day of rest. I stayed at the Best Western Motel. The package with my regalia arrived by 10:00 am. Dave picked me up at noon, and we drove back to Carlyn Park.

D.C., get ready, 'cause here we come.

WASHINGTON, D.C.

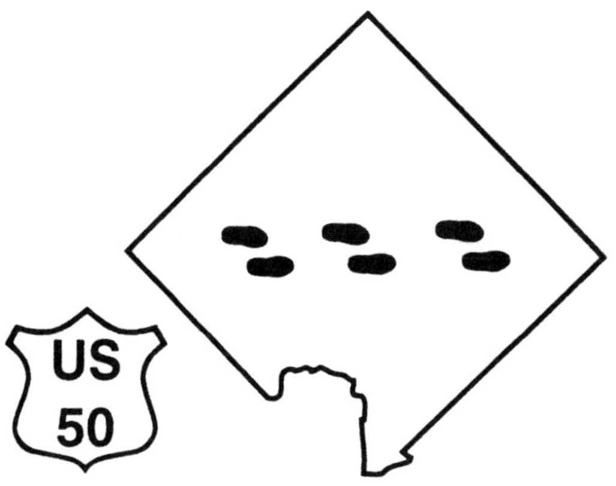

There was a lot of construction along the way and as we walked the last 20 miles into D.C. I could see all the tall buildings, the buildings that housed the U.S. government. It was a very emotional experience for me. I was screaming in my head with triumph, "We made it!" We had walked for five and a half months and covered 3,799 miles. We had just one more mile to go and it would be over. We went to Carlyn Park and spent the night. The next morning most everyone would get into their red shirts, and some of us would dress in our traditional Indian regalia. We would be shuttled from Carlyn Park to Lafayette Park to walk the remaining mile. It was really hard getting to sleep that night. People were talking all-night long, and there were sweats going on. It was all very exciting. Even people who had only walked for two weeks were excited because they knew what we had gone through on our trip from Frisco to D.C. I got a whole three hours sleep and was up at the crack of dawn. For a change, I got to hear the infamous Rooster crow. "Everybody get up for the last mile. One more mile! Everybody get up. You won't have to hear me anymore after today".

That morning everyone was talking amongst themselves, and I was talking with my brother who I had picked up at the airport the day before. We hadn't had much time to talk up to then, and we had a lot to catch up on. He was really glad to be there. He thought it was great to be a part of Indian history. And, we were glad there had been no violence and no mishaps on the entire trip.

At morning circle Dennis let us know we would shuttle to Lafayette Park, and then walk the last mile to LadyBird Johnson Park. They had a stage set up there for Dennis Banks and other speakers, including myself. We saged off and said our prayers, thanking the Creator. We went back and sat around the campfire for about a half-hour before I went and put on my traditional Indian regalia and got ready to walk that last mile. The regalia included a choker, a bear-claw necklace, and moccasins. I would also be wearing three eagle feathers. I went over to where my brother was staying and asked him how I looked. He told me that I looked great.

We parked our vehicles at Lafayette Park and then got organized. We were going to meet up with some Walk for Justice people who had walked up from Florida. Together, we would leave Lafayette Park at 10:00 am and walk into LadyBird Johnson Park to have an all day rally. We formed a last circle and everyone saged off. Dennis spoke, then we all said a prayer and handed out medicine bags to people that had walked. Dave Patton and myself received a Walk for Justice medal.

After we saged off we lined up in an orderly fashion. Dennis Banks was in the front, with three drummers and myself singing the A.I.M. song. Ted Turner and FOX news media were there to film our walk all the way over to LadyBird Johnson Park. The last mile seemed like the longest part of the walk. It just went real slow. It was about 80 degrees and I wasn't even breaking a sweat, even though my traditional regalia was made of elk hide. I was wondering what was going on with my system. Was I just overly excited or what? We had gone about a half-mile when we saw the walkers from Florida coming from the other direction. We could see their red T-shirts.

At the front of the walkers we saw a horse covered with a blanket that said "Free Leonard Peltier". No one was riding the horse, but an Indian in full regalia was escorting it. It was a riderless horse, as if Leonard Peltier was riding it, and it made a strong statement. We shook hands with the Florida walkers and we all got in formation. There were about 150 of the other walkers. Traffic was stopped and people were looking at us. Some had curious looks in their eyes, and some of them had panicked looks like we were reclaiming the land, or something.

It took about an hour and a half to get into LadyBird Johnson Park. We formed one huge spiritual circle where everyone prayed and Dennis told us about the day's scheduled events. The crowd was estimated to be somewhere between 5,000 and 6,000 people. There was no violence, no drinking allowed, and no drugs. There was security to watch our people and keep any onlookers from getting out of hand. The whole rally went very peaceful, without incident.

Dennis was the first speaker. He let everyone know how the Walk for Justice had come about, and how we were making people aware of the fact that Leonard Peltier had suffered a great injustice. He told the crowd what they could do to help Leonard gain his freedom. People were walking through the crowd with petitions to sign. We had collected over 700,000 signatures during the walk, and that didn't count over 20,000 signatures of people from Russia that had been sent to us. Dennis introduced me as one of the Staff carriers, and I spoke to the crowd for two or three minutes about the experience of walking from coast to coast. I told them that we needed to get Leonard Peltier out of prison and that none of us were free until **he** was free. After I spoke, Kris Kristofferson played four songs for everybody, and then the other groups performed. There was a large teepee set up on the grounds and there was a tent that had refreshments.

Dennis informed me that the FBI had paid $2,500 to take out an ad in the Washington Post to present a smear campaign against the American Indian Movement and the Walk for Justice.

The ad, dated July 15, 1994 was a half page and read as follows:

"DEAR MR. PRESIDENT: LEONARD PELTIER MURDERED TWO FBI AGENTS. HE DESERVES NO CLEMENCY."

"June 26, 1975 was a hot, dusty Thursday on the Pine Ridge Indian Reservation in southwestern South Dakota when two young FBI agents arrived from their office in Rapid City. It was about noon when Special Agents Ronald A. Williams, 27, and Jack R. Coler, 28, pulled into the Jumping Bull Compound area of the remote reservation seeking to arrest a young man in connection with the recent abduction and assault of two young ranchers in nearby Manderson, S.D.

Spotting a red and white Chevrolet Suburban van in which they believed the fugitive suspect to be riding, the two agents pursued it toward an open grassy bowl-like area. . ."

They continued to review the case with such a **distorted** portrayal of the facts, I was enraged. Mostly because the misinformation would be believed by those that were unaware of what truly happened. The FBI had more credibility and influence than the American Indian Movement. After all it was a government agency - and what had they done for Indians in the past? In their appeal to the President, after dramatically painting a sordid picture of Leonard, they finished their plea with the following:

"Mr. President, on many occasions you have described this country's law enforcement officers as heroes and heroines. You have said that we must work together to ensure that hardened criminals who prey on the innocent receive punishment commensurate with the harm -- physical, emotional and financial that they have inflicted. We agree.

Mr. President, it's time for Leonard Peltier to pay up. Our judicial system is overwhelmed, overworked and has spoken in this case, again and again. It's time to move on. Leonard Peltier is a vicious, violent and cowardly criminal who hides behind legitimate Native American issues. Leonard Peltier was never a leader in the Native American community. Peltier is simply a vicious thug and murderer with no respect or regard for human life, especially when law enforcement officers are involved. Our citizens, on and off the reservations, must be protected from predators such as Peltier. Our laws must be respected and obeyed or the penalty must be paid. The punishment must also fit the crime -- and it does here.

Mr. President, since Leonard Peltier couldn't fool the federal courts, he is now trying to fool you and the public. He is shading and hiding the facts -- and playing on sympathy. Don't let him get away with it, Mr. President. Sympathy is appropriate only for the dead heroes and their surviving families. Don't let their sacrifice be forgotten."

The Federal Bureau of Investigation Agents Association, P.O. Box 250, New Rochelle, NY 10801

This entire ad was clearly meant to destroy our efforts and attempt to take the public outcry for justice and focus only negative attention on Leonard. So much of this was untrue, blended in with facts, it made for interesting reading to those that didn't know the truth.You would think from reading the ad Leonard was a serial killer! How disappointing it was to see the reaction or lack of response from the media.

When I read the ad, every single mile I had just walked flashed before me. All the obstacles, sore feet, altitude sickness on Monarch Pass, hot asphalt stretching before me. Then I thought of Leonard, him paying for something he didn't do. He had already served 18 years, and if this convinced the President, he would never live to see freedom. Then I thought of Leonard's mother, and the pledge I made to do what ever it took to help get Leonard out. Right then, while the anger built up in me, I started to pray. I prayed that the Creator would intervene and help us to see that justice was done. I prayed that Leonard would receive clemency. I prayed that the Walk For Justice would reach its goal and receive the awareness that we walked for. My eyes were wet by the time I finished my prayer.

The FBI knew what a travesty it was to put Leonard Peltier in the position he has been in for almost 20 years, putting him in prison for something he didn't do. I understood now why we got coverage from many major newspapers during our walk, but when we got to D.C. we had very little newspaper coverage, and that was negative towards us. It shows you what the FBI is capable of doing. The only TV interview we had was with the local FOX affiliate and that was for about two minutes.

Everybody was angry that the FBI went out of their way to place the ad. They did a good job at seeing we got very little media attention, after all the miles we had walked. Dennis got on the PA system and made it known to the whole crowd what the FBI had done. Everyone started booing and yelling "down with the FBI", but nothing got out of hand. The ad was very upsetting to us, but in a strange way, it made us feel good that the FBI felt like they had to spend the time and money to put it in the paper. In a way it was a good sign, and we felt like we had them scared because we had this much support. We had suspected all along that they had planted an agent or two on the Walk for Justice, and this confirmed it.

Dennis told everyone that we would be going over to the Senate building, and he said that anyone who wanted to speak about any of the grievances should be ready at 9:00 in the morning. So, the last day of the walk - July 15, 1994 - was officially over, but the Walk had not come to a conclusion yet, because we still had unfinished business. We still would be talking to Senators and various people who were interested in the case and had the power to recommend executive clemency for Leonard Peltier.

Everyone went back to the campsite about 20 miles away, where we talked about how the day went. I did get a chance to catch up with my brother and talk with him some more. I went to bed knowing that tomorrow we would be at the Senate, speaking up for Leonard Peltier and voicing the grievances. And, I would be one more day closer to home and my wife.

We thought that we had heard the last of it, but the next morning we got up to one last day of the Rooster call. We had a morning circle and saged off, as we had for the past six months.

This was kind of a bittersweet day for me. I had set out in San Francisco to walk for a couple of weeks, which had become a month, and then I had come to the realization that I had to go the whole distance — for Leonard Peltier, for my people, and for myself. Now, I was on a natural high knowing that Creator had let me complete this 3,800-mile journey. I was glad that it was over, but in a sense I felt like it was a new beginning for me. I had found myself on this Walk for Justice, and had left the person that I used to be somewhere out on Highway 50.

I felt like a snake that had shed its skin, and as my friend, Manny Twofeathers says in <u>Stone People Medicine</u>, "Snake helps you release your old life and start anew." One part of my life had ended, and I was looking forward to the rest of it. With Creator's guidance I wanted to help my people, I wanted to help my family, and I wanted to help myself. I realized that we, as Indian people, are more introverted and always

189

the last to speak up for ourselves. I wanted to be a voice. We are more invisible than other peoples of the world. I wanted to be a presence. I realized on the Walk for Justice that I could not let anyone forget what had been done to us. I could no longer let people forget about the injustices done to my people. I wanted to be a thorn in the side, and a constant, visible reminder that we are still here, and still strong.

The next day we all got into vehicles and went back into D.C., to the Senate building. There was plenty of security and they made us go through metal detectors. It wasn't necessary for us, but as far as they were concerned, it was. They had their opinion and we had ours. But what mattered most was, the Indians were in the Senate. We would be heard.

We had 100 people in the Senate room and Dennis Banks was going to be the first speaker. I looked around and there were a lot of empty chairs where various Senators were supposed to be seated. We had heard that there were going to be about 20 Senators, but as I looked around to the side where they were suppose to sit - THERE WERE ONLY THREE PEOPLE. I figured that everyone had gotten a late start, because I just couldn't believe that we had walked all this way to speak our grievances to three people. About an hour went by, and the speaker in the Senate got up and told us that certain Senators wouldn't be showing up, and gave us various reasons. Everyone was starting to get upset. I could feel the fury building up in my throat. Over all the months of walking, being away from home and sacrificing for the cause, I had maintained control. I tried to keep the focus of a spiritual walk, and be positive. But this was just too much to bear.

Dennis got up and spoke to the three Senators that were there, out of the 20 that were supposed to have shown up. You could see the look of anger and disappointment on Dennis Banks' face. What could you say when you had a 90% no show. He made it a point to let the three Senators know what he had to say. Maybe the word would get back to the people who didn't show, and they would find out that they had missed something. But then again, maybe they just didn't care that an **Indian** had been behind bars, unjustly, for all this time. Maybe they didn't care that we had all these grievances to bring to light. Maybe they didn't care about violating the civil rights of the **Red** Man. Maybe they just didn't care at all.

Dennis Banks spoke for about an hour. He had told me earlier that I would be speaking after him, but when we took a break I told him that I didn't think I should speak due to the frame of mind I was in. I was so mad, and I was worried that if I got up to speak I would hurt a lot of white people's feelings, white people who had walked with us and helped us bring our cause to light. And I knew that would not do our cause any good. So, I declined to speak.

We spent about three hours with the three Senators, and all of our concerns and grievances were covered, but during those three hours I saw one of the Senators dozing off. I wanted to go over there and just scream in his face and tell him to wake up. **This was no joke**. At least it wasn't to us. The only Senator who had anything positive to say about our cause was Ben Nighthorse Campbell, who is American Indian himself.

The ones who were there did hear what we had to say, and we figured that was better than nothing. I told Dennis that we had done the whole walk peacefully and no one had gotten hurt, and there were no racial incidents that amounted to anything. I remember when we took over the B.I.A. building in 1972; we got response because of the threat of violence. On the peaceful Walk for Justice we got no response. I wondered what we had to do to get someone's attention.

After the hearings, people were not in the best of moods. Everyone was saying their good-byes out in the hall. I went with Dennis and his family to one of the vehicles. I gave him a hug and said I would see him at the Sundance next month. After that, my brother and I discussed how angry we were that no one had showed up. I told him that it goes to show you how the long arm of the FBI can scare people off.

Dave Patton and his family took me to the airport an hour later so I could catch my plane back to Las Vegas. Going past the Congress building I thought of the walk.

We had put our hearts and souls into that 3,800-mile Walk, made millions of people across the country aware of the cause, got thousands of signatures on petitions, and ended the Walk for Justice by talking to **THREE PEOPLE**.

The Walk was over, and the natural thing to do was wonder if it was all worth it. There were many days when, physically and emotionally, I didn't feel like I could walk another step. Other days I didn't **want** my feet to move because of the pain from having blisters on top of blisters. Some days I had to use duct tape to keep the skin on my feet when bandages weren't enough. I would ask myself why I was putting myself through all this mental and physical punishment. And then there were days when I was just grateful to be alive and free to enjoy the beauty and majesty of the earth. I had become a spiritual person on the Walk, and I will always be grateful for that. And the Walk had done a lot to physically prepare me for the Sundance as well. It had strengthened me and helped with my endurance. Walking with the Eagle Staff everyday helped me be strong, and I knew that this strength was not of myself. It was a gift from Creator. He gave me the strength and the will to put one foot in front of the other for 3,800 miles. He kept me healthy. He kept me safe.

There were other positives as a result of the Walk for Justice. We got the word out to millions of people through the media. An awareness of Leonard Peltier's case exists where there was no knowledge before. The nuclear waste dump was not put on the Ponca Reservation, most likely as a result of our Walk. People were told about the injustices **still** being done to American Indian peoples; how land is still being stolen, how rights are still taken away, how treaties still don't seem to mean anything, and how things are still being dumped on us because no one cares.

I only pray and hope that you do.

BACK HOME

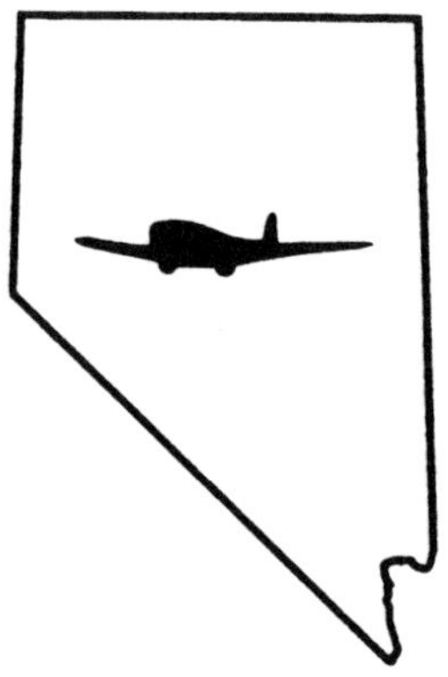

As the plane was taking off I looked out over the city that houses and symbolizes our government and realized that I loved to hate the place. I just thought to myself, "Good old D.C." I felt mad, hurt, betrayed, and disgusted-all at the same time. We were in the air for about 20 minutes, and I hoped that if I ever had to come back to this place it would be for positive reasons, and with better results.

On the flight home it only took me five hours to fly over the same area that it had taken me six months to walk across. As the plane was flying over Colorado, the pilot came on the intercom and informed the passengers we were passing over Monarch Pass. I thought to myself, "Been there, done that." I looked over at the passenger sitting next to me and was going to tell him I crossed over the pass on foot in a blizzard, but I'm sure his reaction would be yeah, right! All in all I was happy knowing that this endeavor was over, even though I knew it wouldn't really be over until Leonard Peltier was released from jail. I knew that we had done everything we could. And I knew that, somehow, we would do more. It wasn't over yet.

I was very happy to land in Las Vegas, and I was **really** happy to see my wife. The feeling that I had when I threw my arms around her was even better than it had been when I imagined it, mile after lonely mile. It was so good to see her, and so good to realize what we had done together as a team. Without her support I couldn't have done what I did. I loved her with all my heart when I left, and I somehow felt even closer to her now.

It was a relief to finally be at the place that I called home; a place that didn't have to be taken down and moved everyday. We picked up my luggage and got on the road, going down the strip back to my apartment. The city looked really crowded to me, and I knew that it would take me a while before I blended back into Las Vegas.

Now that the Walk was over I had to get myself back into a rhythm. One of the first things I did was unpack my backpack and look at the various mementos I had picked up along the way. I looked at one particular stick I had found on Alcatraz Island that I had carried with me every day, and decided to make it a part of my regalia. It was a piece of Mother Earth and I had carried it all the way on the walk, so I decided to make it into a staff and put a bald eagle's head on the top of it. I thought that maybe I could pass the staff down, and people would say, "This is the stick that your grandfather found on Alcatraz Island when he started the Walk for Justice". The stick is about five feet long, and when I looked back at pictures taken along the way, all it had on it was one bald eagle feather. When I got my walking stick back from the taxidermist with the bald eagle head on it, it looked beautiful. I put three additional eagle feathers on it, and a medicine bag. Then I had it blessed. I hold it very sacred.

For quite some time I was lonesome for the freedom of the road. It took awhile to unwind and get back to the hustle and bustle of city life, and I found out that I wasn't the only one that felt that way. I would talk on the phone with other walkers, and they were having a hard time adjusting back into city life. Over and over I would hear about missing Highway 50 and how good we had it. Then, slowly but surely the calls subsided, and I knew that it was a sign that people were blending back into the city. Adjusting was good, but I sure hoped that no one would ever forget what the Walk had meant, what it stood for.

I stayed in touch with a handful of people after that. Dave Patton and his family had settled in California, and we agreed to get together for a pow wow in San Diego. My wife and I drove down, and we were sitting in the bleachers in the arena, watching the Indian people dance, when I saw Dave and his family looking around for us. I wondered if they had managed to adjust to the city. We spent the day together and had a great time. I told him I would stay in touch, and he said to make sure I told him how things went at the Sundance.

We went back home, and I began to make my final preparations. The Walk was over; the Sundance was about to begin. Ho! Mitakuye Oyasin! (All My Relations)

THE SUNDANCE

I called Dennis Banks and spoke with his daughter Glenda, regarding my skirt for the Sundance. I told her that I would give her two eagle feathers in return for making the skirt. When the day came, I flew to Minnesota and stayed at Dennis Banks' daughter's house, and it felt like the old Walk for Justice again. Dennis and about 40 other people from the Walk were there. I spent a day with them, and then we left for the Sundance in Pipestone.

We had a great night, staying up to the late hours, singing spiritual Indian songs, and we had a Sweat Lodge at the end of the night. It was good to see everyone. I felt like we were back on Highway 50 again.

The next morning we headed out for Pipestone, which was about a six or seven hour drive from where we were. We had a great time going down the road, singing Indian songs and drumming. After a couple of hours Dennis had us stop. He knew where there was a lot of sage that we could get, and we all picked several plastic bags full. I had never picked sage before, but I found out that this is something they did every year on the way to the Sundance.

As we pulled into Pipestone we saw this welcome sign, and in the distance I could see several painted tepees off in the meadows. It was like being shot back in time. There were approximately 20 that were painted in all different colors. It was something to see all these tepees sitting in the meadow, where people had been Sundancing for hundreds of years, before the white people outlawed it. This particular place was a relatively new location. It had just been OK'd to hold Sundances here, and this was only the fifth year they had done it. We got to the Sundance area and quickly found out that there was a lot of security. They all knew Dennis Banks, so we were "In like Flint."

We set up our tents wherever we wanted to. Anyone who was not Sundancing set up their tents outside the fence which surrounded the tepees. I chose a teepee with a wolf painted on it. Some had Buffalo, one had a bear, and they all were painted with different animals. I stashed my gear and set up my sleeping bag. When I laid down, I looked up and thought, "Wow! This is a real teepee". I felt closer to Mother Earth now, more than ever, being in this teepee.   I wondered how it had been for Indian brothers in past times: How had they made it through the winter, and how hot they must have gotten in the summer. I was kind of lost in my thoughts when I heard a knock on the lodge pole. Someone told me that we all needed to help construct the arbor, the place where people watching the Sundance would sit. So, we went out and cut down some Aspen and Willow to put on top of the Sundance arbor.

It went around in a half circle, and it was about 10 feet high. We would be putting chicken wire over the top of 2X4's and laying the branches on top of that for shade. Everybody was there helping, as the Sundance was just two days away. We also had a long day of cutting wood for the sweats we would be having during the Sundance.

I had a real good sense of freedom, being out in the open with my Indian brothers and sisters. It was almost like being back on Highway 50. But, this was about the Sundance, and this was something that I had wanted to do for a long time. During the next two days people came in from all over. We had people from Canada and all 50 states. We had some people come in from France that were interested in the Sundance religion. It wasn't a carnival atmosphere by any means. Everyone knew it was a very sacred area and there was to be no alcohol or drugs allowed. Security was to make sure that no people came in to cause any trouble, and no one was allowed to take pictures. As Indian people, we invite all races to come to the Sundance to observe and see this holy and sacred rite.

At Pipestone they don't allow anyone but American Indians to dance. Some Sundances vary from state to state. My personal belief is that the Sundance should stay Indian because it is a religion that has been around for thousands of years, and it's the only thing that hasn't been taken away from us. However, I believe that non-Indians should be able to come to watch, observe, and see what it's all about.

I met some great people during the time we were setting up, and one Indian guy I met was a Lakota Sioux named Owns a Saber. He had been a Sundancer for 14 years. He took a particular liking to me, especially after he found out it would be my first time Sundancing. It was a camaraderie thing to tease the first-timers, give them somewhat of a hard time, and guide them at the same time. But, it's always fun to be a newcomer so the experienced ones can tease you and put the fear into you. Owns a Saber gave me a lot of advice and told me that he was in his 50's and had a bum leg, and he was going to do his 15th Sundance.

He wanted to know if I could move from sunup to sundown, and if I could run 28 miles a day, because that was what it was like. Of course, I knew I had just come off the Walk for Justice and I knew what I could do. But, he got me pointed in the right direction. Like telling me about putting two small stones in my mouth for moisture. Also, he told me to pace myself and pray hard while I was Sundancing. He said, "Pray for everybody, all your relations, and pray for yourself last and you'll make it through."

I ended up helping him make his pegs for the Sundance. He had a whole bag of pegs, which were about four inches long, and I had to whittle them down on both ends for him. He was an Elder, and I felt privileged to help him get these pegs ready for all the Sundancers. He made sure I had an eagle bone whistle and a pipe. During our conversation we talked about Dennis Banks and he found out that I was on the Walk for Justice. He asked me how far I had walked and I told him, "I went the whole way". He shook my hand and said that he was proud of me. We talked about Leonard Peltier and how we both hoped that he would get out of prison soon. We would both pray hard for him.

The day before the Sundance I went into town and called my wife. I told her I wouldn't able to talk to her during the next four days because I couldn't leave the grounds. I told her I would let her know as soon as I was finished, if I had made it or didn't make it. This would be the last phone call for four days. She said she loved me and she would be praying for me. She told me my brother would be praying for me, too.

The town of Pipestone was kind of small, but I went and found a place to buy several bottles of Welch's Grape juice and some other liquids. Owns a Saber told me to drink as much liquid as possible, because I wouldn't be drinking anything for four days once the Sundance started. So, I loaded up my cooler, knowing it would be taken out of the teepee once we started. After all, you're out there for pain and suffering. I wanted to make sure I had plenty of liquids inside me, but they told me not to get sodas, because they dehydrate you.

When I got back to the Sundance area I started helping the people that were getting the grounds ready. I ran into Dennis Banks and he told me that Glenda had my skirt and it was ready. It was bright red with an eagle on the back, and it had blue trim around the edges. It was colorful, and I thanked her for making it for me. I still had to make my crown of sage and some sage wristbands. I had been told that I should make those the night before so they wouldn't dry out on me. I went to see Owns A Saber, who was sitting in his teepee eating a big submarine sandwich. He told me I should fatten myself up like the brown bears do because I wasn't going to be eating or drinking anything for four days.

That night, I went to my teepee about 9:00. It was getting a little cold, so I went and got some wood from where they were having the sweats and started a nice little fire. As I sat there enjoying myself I looked out the door and saw these feet and legs, and heard a voice asking if anyone was in there. It was another Lakota Indian brother who was looking for someone to room with. I told him there was plenty of room. For the Sundance, it's first come, first served, so if all the space is taken, you have to pitch a tent outside the tepees. Dennis had told me to get there early if I wanted to be guaranteed a spot, and I was glad I had taken Dennis' advice.

Everybody in my particular teepee was from the walk, and they were Sundancing for the first time. We expected 200 or 300 spectators of all races. We also expected 200 male Sundancers and 50 women.

The last day before the Sundance we finished up the arbor and set out to get the Sundance tree. We were told that the Sundance Chief was going to select a tree, and then all the able bodied men, women and children would go out and chop that tree down by hand. Then we would carry it back, regardless of how far away it was. There was a hole three feet across and about six feet deep where we would put the Tree of Life down into Mother Earth. It would be the Tree of Life in the center of the arbor. Everyone who was going to pierce would be attaching their ropes to the Tree of Life.

When I say "piercing", what I mean is, incisions are made in the chest of a Sundancer, and a peg, or piercing bone is put through the cuts. Sometimes, more than one peg is used. A rope is connected to the peg that is imbedded in the chest, and that rope runs to and is attached to the Tree of Life.

In a sense, these ropes are like umbilical cords connected to that Tree of Life. The tree is a part of Mother Earth and we're connected as one to Mother Earth. You select a spot on the tree where you want to put your rope, and you have colors on it so you can identify your rope among all the other ropes on the tree. So, when it comes time to get your rope and attach it to the pegs that were embedded into your skin you can easily tell where your rope is. When the proper time comes, the Sundancer must break free by ripping the bones free from the skin-tearing the skin from incision to incision . The Tree of Life is very sacred, and the Sundance is very powerful medicine.

Word got back to the arbor that the Chief had found an Aspen tree about a half-mile away. We were told it was at least two stories high. About a hundred of us took some axes and went down to the tree. At about this time, Leonard Crowdog, who is the medicine man of the Sioux Tribe got into camp. Leonard went with us to bless this tree. We all took towels to use for padding on our shoulders. I was glad I had brought the towel, because carrying the tree was hard enough, without having it rub your shoulders raw.

When we got to this wooded area we saw the tree. It really was two to three stories high. It had a red ribbon tied around it so we would know it was the right one. We saged off, and Leonard Crowdog blessed the tree, the Tree of Life. Then a couple of young Indian brothers climbed to the top of the tree and put ropes around it, so when it started to fall we could control it and it wouldn't fall on anyone. It took about 45 minutes for us to chop the tree to the point where it started to sway and get weak. While we were chopping the tree other people laid down these long 2X4's so the tree would fall on them. People got on each side of these boards. We would support the boards on our shoulders, and this is how we would carry the Tree of Life back to the Sundance area. Once they figured where the tree would be landing they gave it a few more chops. It landed, bulls eye, right on the boards.

The hardest part was getting everybody to lift at the same time, in unison, in order to get it on our shoulders. All the bigger guys were near the front or the back, and the smaller people were in the middle. It took us about an hour and fifteen minutes to get the tree back. It was a great experience to carry the tree back to the Sundance arbor. It was very, very difficult to pick up this tree that weighed hundreds of pounds. Everybody was sweating, but together, we got the tree back to the arbor, laid it down, and lined it up with the hole in the ground. Everybody got on the opposite ends of the ropes and guided it into the hole in Mother Earth.

When that was done, another crew was packing rocks, Pipestone, and dirt into the hole, filling it back up. We all did this, and although it was a tiring and rough experience, everybody pulled together and got it done. Once we got the tree in there, everybody tied their ropes to it, put tobacco ties on their ropes, and said their prayers.

The night before the Sundance everybody had a feast, including the people who wouldn't be dancing but were there to watch. They were cooking all kinds of traditional foods, including fried bread. Someone had donated a hindquarter of elk, and they were making elk stew. There was chili, corn on the cob, and even Kentucky Fried Chicken. We formed a circle and saged off, then lined up for the feast. Dennis told the Sundancers to line up first and then everyone else after them. The Indian women had been cooking for a day and a half, and I ate three or four plates full because I knew I would be going without food and water for four days.

The feast went on until midnight, and the first timers were getting teased. We sat around talking about what it was like to Sundance. I had all my regalia, including my whistle, my Chanupa, my skirt, and my sage crown with two eagle feathers attached, facing Mother Earth. I knew we would be getting up at the crack of dawn for the first Sundance sweat, but I had a hard time getting to sleep. I was anxious, yet there was some apprehension of the unknown. I finally went to sleep around 2:00 in the morning.

I slept very well until I heard a whistle blowing mildly, and I asked what that meant. An Indian brother told me it was time to get up and start the first sweat. It was a ghostly sound, and it sent chills up my spine. I was very honored to hear that sound. I had been waiting for, and preparing for this moment for a long time. I sat up, and everyone started rummaging around, getting their gear ready. We would have a Sweat Lodge to purify ourselves, and then we would come back to the teepee and get into our Sundance regalia. Then we would take our Chanupa's out to the altar and set them down to be blessed, so we could take them into the Sundance arbor with us.

Even though it was August, it was still quite cool out on the plains, and in order to go into the

Sweat Lodge, you would just put a towel around you. Depending on who was saying the prayers, you could be in the Sweat Lodge for five minutes or 15 minutes. Since I didn't like the cold, I was really anxious to get in there and heat up. While I was standing by the fire warming up I was thinking about where I was, and what was taking place. The Lodge Keeper said, "Come on". There were four or five Sweat Lodges and everyone got in line. I said "All my Relations", and I went into the Sweat Lodge.

We prayed for our relations and for our families. We prayed for four rounds and it was over. I went back to my teepee. I got into my regalia and felt proud, thinking about my brothers in the old days getting ready to pray to the Creator. I took my Chanupa over to the altar. Everybody lined their pipes up for a final prayer, before going to the Sundance Altar. As soon as we were ready, the Sundance Chief yelled "Hoca, Hoca, Hoca Hey" which means in Lakota "Let's go. Everybody line up."

We lined up according to how many years we had Sundanced. Those who had Sundanced for 10 years or more were at the front, and five years on down to first year lined up in order. First timers like myself were going last. I had my arms folded, and the pipe was cradled there. There were roughly 150 Indian brothers lined up in their regalia, ready to pay their respects to Mother Earth and to Creator. I had been told by the Elders that as a first timer I should just watch and follow. I put my eagle bone whistle in my mouth and held my pipe across my forearm. We were facing the rising sun. When the Sundance Chief said "Hoca, Hoca, Hoca Hey" again, we all started our movement into the Sundance arbor.

We were blowing our eagle-bone whistles, and prayed to the four directions, North, South, East, and West. When we got to the arbor we lined up in a circle, still blowing our whistles. When the Sundance Chief yelled "Hoca" we all ran to the Tree of Life and found a spot. We put our hands on the tree and kneeled and prayed to Mother Earth. Then we ran back to our designated spot. This would be done four times. Then we paired off and began to dance at our own pace.

We blew our whistles in unison. Sundance songs were being sung. The drums were powerful and they gave me drive and strength. I looked around at all my Indian brothers and sisters, and it made my heart feel good to know that I was finally out here with all my people; that my journey had come full circle. I kept saying to myself "I'm finally here."

We rotated around the Tree of Life four times and we kept blowing our whistles, almost in a trance-like state. The main thing I had been told was that in the Sundance you had to pace yourself so you didn't burn out. I felt good and strong and my heart felt happy. I was very emotional, and I felt lifted. I felt very spiritual. For the first time in my 43 years I found myself crying without shame, and for me to cry was a great release. Tears were falling down on Mother Earth. She was saying to me, "You need to do this.

It's alright to humble yourself to Mother Earth." It was like taking a hundred-pound weight off my back. I was feeling the best I had felt in my life in the first half-hour. I can only tell you it was a phenomenal feeling.

I quickly found out that walking and dancing on the grass in Pipestone is almost like walking on porcupine quills or straw. Everyone was barefoot and we were dancing on Mother Earth. The energies were coming through. Some Sundances allow you to wear Moccasins, but it wasn't allowed at Pipestone. I soon found out that these little, bitty rocks and the grass became very irritating and painful on your feet. I had to block this out, because I was only a little way into the Sundance and it was going to get worse before it got better. I was looking up toward the sun and praying hard, thinking about all those miles and all those months praying for my mother and father, praying for my wife, praying for my brothers. I was praying hard. I was praying for forgiveness for all the wrong I had done to anybody. I was praying to be a better person. I was praying for everybody. I was praying for Leonard Peltier. All my friends and all my relations. I prayed for everyone I had ever known. Anyone I could think of. The past up to the present was going through my mind. It felt good to be praying for these people. I felt that this would reach them somehow.

I kept blowing my eagle-bone whistle. I was strong, and all the other Sundancers were dancing hard and strong. The drums were sounding better and better, and they made me dance harder and harder. The first few hours I kept the rhythm going, pacing myself. I was already thinking about that cold grape juice I had on ice. I was already thinking about water, and how good it would be to have that gift from Mother Earth, knowing that neither beast nor man can survive without it. If everybody in the world were to Sundance, water would become so precious to them. I don't think you would see the waste and pollution that we have going on now. That entered my mind at various times, how shameful and bad it is that people do wrong things to Mother Earth. You just don't know what you've got till it's gone, or till you can't have it. Leonard Peltier would like to be here feeling the pain and the hunger and the thirst that I would feel over the next four days. I had to block these things out of my mind and be strong.

It felt good to be with sharing this ceremony with my past spirit-brother Sundancers, like Red Cloud and Crazy Horse. I imagined them in their day, and experienced the feeling of being a part of that spiritual bonding with the past and present Sundancers. I felt so much closer to Mother Earth and my people when we were all dancing out there together, dancing as one. One whistle, one heartbeat, one movement. Several times I saw the people watching under the Sundance arbor and wished I was with them in the shade. But, this was about pain and suffering. I could see people from all races there to watch the Sundance. There were Indians, white people, black people, asian people, and people from other races. It made me feel good to know that these people were taking an interest in the Sundance.

At times, I would move my eyes to see how everyone else was doing, and one time I saw Owns a Saber. I was surprised to see how well he was moving for a man his age, bum leg and all. I wished I had become a Sundancer 10 or 15 years earlier. At 43 I wasn't a spring chicken but for my age I was in pretty good shape. There were people of all ages in the Sundance circle, including some young boys that were 9, 10, and 11, all the way up to one Elder who, I believe, was in his mid 70's. I had no reason to feel old, and it didn't matter that I hadn't done this earlier. My time was **now,** and that's what I was focusing on. Creator had chosen this time for me, and I was grateful.

Women danced behind us for support, and they ranged in age from 19 to 65. They danced behind us, blowing their whistles, dancing, and fanning us off. They danced just as hard as the men did. Women have that energy, and they can take more pain and suffering. You have to be proud of them, giving us that support.

As I danced I wondered how I was going to pierce, from the back or the front. If I pierced from the back it meant I would have to pull seven buffalo skulls. There would be one skull for each of the Four Directions, one skull for Mother Earth, one skull for Father Sky, and one skull for Creator. You pull these skulls around the arbor until you break free. The other way to pierce is from the front, where you would run back from the Tree of Life and pull yourself free. It wasn't about which one was easier or which one I wanted to do; it was all about what would be the best for the needs of my people. I decided to consult with the Sundance Chief regarding my choice.

The first day was really hard. In all my thinking about it, though, I never did think it was going to be easy. Other people who had danced two, three, or four Sundances told me that the problem wasn't the first or second day. It's usually the third day and the fourth day that really gets you. That's why you must pace yourself and not take anything for granted. I prayed hard all day, and before I knew it the sun in front of us was now behind us, and it was going down. It was dusk. Everybody repeated at the end what they had done at the beginning. When the Sundance Chief said "Hoca Hey", everybody ran to the Tree of Life, touched it, and said their final prayer. We went back to our tepees and prepared for the Sweat Lodge at the day's end, so we could relax our muscles. You could go into as many Sweat Lodges as you wanted. You could do whatever you wanted with your free time - except eat or drink.

I quickly decided to get my muscles revitalized in the hot Sweat Lodge and then go right to bed. I prayed and thanked the Creator for a good day of dancing for myself and the rest of my brothers and sisters. I then went back to my teepee with sore feet, and cracked, dry lips. I figured the sooner I went back to my teepee and went to sleep, the less I would think about food and water.

I woke up to the eagle-bone whistle and heard the phrase "Hoca Hey". On the morning of the second day I felt slow and groggy. The muscles in my legs, and actually in my whole body, were sore. I didn't know how much strength I had, but I figured I would leave that problem for the Creator. I headed for the Sweat Lodge, where we sang prayer songs and thanked the Creator for the second day of Sundancing.

We left the Sweat Lodge and got into our regalia, getting ready for the second day. I spoke with Dennis Banks' nephew, Alex Tenbears, about not knowing whether I wanted to pierce from the back or the front. He suggested I go to the Sundance Chief and offer him some tobacco, smoke the pipe with him, and ask for his advice. I went to the Sundance Chief and he asked me what I was praying for. I told him there was a lot of alcoholism and sickness in my family, and told him my father had been an alcoholic for 30 years. He suggested I pull the skulls, because that's done for sickness and to cure the people you're praying for. After talking to the Sundance Chief, Harry Bird, I felt that's what I should do. I would pierce from behind and pull the seven skulls.

I would be pulling the skulls around the arbor, which was about the size of a soccer field, around the Tree of Life, and around the other Sundancers. There would be four staffs signifying the Four Directions, and each would have a color; red, yellow, black, and white. I would have to pull the skulls around after pegs were attached through incisions in my skin. I would take a rope off the Tree of Life, attach it to the Buffalo skulls, and then attach them to the piercing bones in my back. I would pull them behind me, around the arbor four times, for each direction. They are very heavy. Each skull weighs about 35 or 40 pounds - times seven. You can figure out from that how heavy they were.

The Sundance is not to see how strong you are mentally or physically. This was a spiritual ceremony, and I felt I was going to be able to do what I came here to do. If I failed, I would have to wait until the next year. There are people who come out with good intentions who just can't make it. If I did fail, it would not be the first time someone had failed, or the last, but I felt the time was now. I knew I would be piercing from behind, and pulling the skulls for my family.

I wondered if I would have the courage to pierce. I felt somewhat alone out there, even though I was with my Indian brothers and sisters. I realized none of my family was there with me, but I knew I would be strong enough to pierce when my time came. It was for them. It was for "All my relations". **That** would give me the courage and strength I needed.

We heard "Hoca Hey", and everybody got excited. We all asked how everyone was doing, and we were all doing okay. We lined up and danced out to the Sundance Arbor. I wound up in the same spot

I had danced in the first day. I could see people were moving a little slower than they did the first day.

The other people were feeling like I did. We were trying to get into the mood and the feeling. But, before you knew it, the sound of the drums and the whistles got everyone going. After a half-hour, everyone was dancing hard and in rhythm. I prayed hard to the Creator, knowing I had not decided whether to pierce on the second or the third day. I figured I would leave it up to the Creator to guide me.

I continued to dance, but couldn't help thinking about water. I was really thirsty and kept thinking about that cold bottle of grape juice in the cooler. I kept thinking about how nice it would be to have a cool glass of water. I knew other people were feeling the same way. After all, you can't live without water.

There would be a handful of people piercing today, and I could see some of the dancers with circles on their chests. This is where they would be pierced. I had never been to a Sundance before, but I knew to pray for the people who would be pierced this day.

I saw the Sundance Chief grab one of the Sundancers by his sage wristband and lead him around the arbor to the Tree of Life. The Sundancer kneeled down and prayed. There was a buffalo robe by the Tree of Life, stretched out on sage. No one had told me what that was about. I watched as he laid down on the buffalo robe after being led around the arbor.

Two other Sundance Chiefs came out and rubbed his back with sage. He took off his sage crown and put it in his mouth. I could see they were cutting his skin so they could put the piercing peg in his wounds, to hook him up on his rope to the Tree of Life. I was really surprised that this Sundance brother didn't even move, or yell, or anything. He stood up and went to the Tree, found his rope and hooked himself up to the ends, and then danced away from the Tree of Life. He did this four times, stretching his skin out. He was getting ready to pull himself free and tear the piercing peg out of the skin on his chest. I watched him pull back and stretch his skin out to make it easier to break free on the fourth run back. I knew what was going to happen, I expected what was going to happen, but it still shocked me to see him run out to the end of the rope, and to hear the popping sound of the skin when the piercing pegs tore through his chest. I saw the rope flying through the air with pieces of skin on the peg.

I lost my rhythm for a minute. I was amazed how fast he had pierced and how fast he broken loose. I didn't even want to think about my time after what I had just seen. It didn't look barbaric, but it wasn't something you see everyday. I would be lying if I said it didn't scare me even more than I already was, but I knew the Creator would see me through.

Other Sundance brothers pierced throughout the day, on and off, and before we knew it, another day had come to an end. We headed to the Sweat Lodge and then back to our tepees. I told Tenbears that I wasn't going to lie, and the sound of the pegs popping out of the skin of the chest scared the hell out of me.

It made me nervous, but I was making this commitment for life. Once a Sundancer, always a Sundancer. I wasn't going to change my mind just because I had seen a little blood. Another Sundancer who had been pierced twice before assured me I would have the strength by the time I was called out there before the Tree of Life. He said the Creator would help me, and he told me to not worry about it.

I laid back and watched the fire in the teepee, looking out the top of the teepee at the stars and wondering how my ancestors who were Sundancers had handled this situation in the past. I decided right then and there that I would pierce tomorrow - the third day. It would be my day to come before the Creator and become a Sundancer.

I woke up the next morning ready to go. I had made up my mind. I went to the Sundance Chief and told him I would be piercing today. He told everyone who was piercing that day to get in line so they could be marked. He marked my back with buffalo fat and drew two brown circles where they were going to pierce me. I was coming close to the time I was looking for. We had our sweat and then found ourselves in the Sundance Arbor dancing. We were all getting tired, but I thanked the Creator for keeping me strong, and continued to dance.

Before I knew it, my time had come. The next thing I knew I was being led around the arbor by my sage wristband to the buffalo robe. I was laying on my stomach thinking, "This is really intense". I'm not going to say that I wasn't scared, because I was. I'm not going to say that I wasn't nervous, because I was. I took off my sage crown and put it in my mouth. As I looked around, I could see Leonard Crowdog walking out from under the arbor, and I wondered what I had done to deserve this. Among Sundance people he is considered a very holy man, and he is known for piercing deep. I had heard horror stories about his deep piercing. But, when I saw him, I was proud to know that I was being pierced by Leonard Crowdog. I was scared, but I knew I could handle it.

The next thing I knew, Crowdog was leaning beside me and wiping my back with some disinfectant. I could feel my flesh being cut on one side and there was a real sharp pain. Then I was cut on the other side. It hurt, but I can say I really didn't feel much pain after the first cut. I could feel the pegs sliding through the holes in my skin, in through one end and out the other, where they were being secured. Then Leonard Crowdog told me to stand up, and the ropes were attached to each peg in my back. The Sundance Chief danced over to me and said, "When you're ready, let me know". I nodded my head and danced over to the skulls. He said, "When you see this eagle feather go up in the air it is the signal for you to start pulling". I went to my spot, and I heard the Sundance Chief say "Hoca, Hoca Hey" and I took off, pulling the skulls.

It was a real strange feeling. Even though these were sacred buffalo skulls and this was the Sundance, I felt just like I was working hard to stay strong. But

I was a Sundancer pulling these skulls over the ground at the Sundance to prepare for healing and change to come to my people. It was very hard pulling them over the ground. They still had their teeth, and the teeth were sticking in the ground. I could see the Sundance Chief along side me saying "Hoca Hoca." "Let's go." I was blowing my whistle and pulling the skulls. It seemed like an eternity going around the arbor four times. I was breathing hard and was so dry, drier than I could ever imagine. Even in my worst nightmare.

This was the third day without food or water and I was relatively weak. I had to stop at each marker facing the four directions and pray. I prayed for all my relations, and to the Creator to keep me strong, because it was getting harder by the second, and I needed all His help to get me around the arbor. By now I was breathing and panting hard. My mouth was very dry and my lips were chapped. It almost felt like I was foaming at the mouth from exhaustion.

Thoughts about the Walk for Justice went through my mind. I realized that the 3,800 miles had prepared me for the physical part of the Sundance. There was just no way to prepare for the combination of physical pain, mental exhaustion, and deprivations that could only be experienced at Sundance.

I finally got around the arbor, and it was time for me to break free. My skin had been stretched from pulling the skulls, but it would not let go of the pegs — it would not tear. The Sundance Chief stopped me. He took one adult and two children and put them on the buffalo skulls so they would remain stationary. He said that when he yelled "Hoca" I was to back up all the way to the buffalo skulls and I was to take off running, trying to break free. It was becoming a tug of war between my skin and the buffalo skulls. I backed up to the skulls and took off running. My mind was in slow motion. There was about 30 feet of rope, and when I hit the end of it, it was like a bungee cord had been attached to my skin. It yanked me back, lifted me off the ground, and body slammed me. It knocked the wind out of me and knocked the sage crown off my head. I put the crown back on and got up, struggling to get my breath back.

I could hear the people go "Oooh" and I could see them praying for me. I could see the pain and frustration in their eyes because I hadn't broke free. The Sundance Chief told me I would have to do it again. I backed up and then took off running for all I was worth, and it was a carbon copy of the first time. I lifted off the ground and got body slammed into the earth again. It knocked the wind out of me, and I thought to myself, "What did I do to deserve this?" I was starting to have doubts.

The Sundance Chief came over and helped me up, and said he was going to get two big guys out here to run with me, one on each side. Also, they were going to put another child on the skulls to keep them stationary. I looked out and could see Clyde Bellecourt, who weighs about 230 pounds, and another Indian brother who weighed about the same. They said, "Come on brother. We know it's hard, but we're going to help you". We backed up, and when the Sundance Chief said "Hoca" all three of us took off running fast, with them holding onto my arms. My left side broke free, but the right side was still attached.

We went back to the skulls and repeated what we had just done. I was still attached. I broke free on the fifth try, and the rope went flying. When I broke free I was dazed, but I still could hear all the people in the arbor cheering, happy with relief. To my amazement, the Sundance Chief grabbed my sage wristband and ran me around the Four Directions and over to the Tree of Life. He raised his eagle fan up and said, "The skin didn't break, the peg did". I had to go back and have a new peg put in again. This time I was numb. I couldn't feel the peg sliding into my skin. I went back to the skulls and they tied the rope to it. Clyde Bellecourt and the other Sundancer came out to run with me again, and on the sixth try, my skin tore and the piercing bone finally came free.

I had just enough energy to be lead around the Sundance arbor and make it back to my spot. I was lightheaded and dizzy, and thought I was going to pass out. I prayed hard to the Creator to make me strong again, to get me to the fourth day. I started to feel better about that time. The Sundancer next to me had an eagle feather in his hand, pointed toward the sky. Everyone else was looking up, and I called up the strength to look up and see what was going on. There were two golden eagles flying above us, three or four hundred feet up in the air.

Everybody started blowing their whistles, and that was just what I needed to keep going. It brought tears to my eyes and got us all through the third day with ease after seeing the golden eagles. They came to us when I finally broke free.

The piercing continued throughout the day, and that night we went to the Sweat Lodges and prayed. I had medicine put on my wounds and although I was accustomed to sleeping on my back, I knew I would be sleeping on my stomach that night. When I got to my teepee, all my Indian brothers came by and told me I was strong. One after the other, they came and shook my hand. It made me feel proud and I thanked the Creator for getting me through the day. As I laid there I thought, "I would just love to drink a whole gallon of water or iced tea."

Everybody was wondering how long the Sundance would last the next day, and who still had to pierce. Although the Sundance was supposed to last from sunup to sundown, usually on the last day, when everybody is done piercing, it could end at 5:00 instead of 6:00. Then we could feast and put food and water back into our systems. One guy sharing the teepee, named Jerry Yellow Thunder, told me he had been coming out for the past five years. He said the eagles come at least one day during the Sundance every year. I was amazed to know that these birds had showed up every year since they made the Sundance legal at Pipestone.

I was really looking forward to dancing tomorrow, now that I had made it through some of the hardest parts. I was feeling better mentally, but being a Sundancer is never over. It's not just the piercing; it's what you believe and how you carry that spirituality. I was happy I had pierced on the third day, and tomorrow was the fourth day. We would all have a good dance, and we would have a feast. Next I would be going to Wisconsin to attend two pow wows, and then home to Las Vegas.

The next morning we got up for the fourth and final day, and everyone was in really good spirits. My back was really in pain and my legs were hurting, but it was the final day, and that gave me the strength to go on. It would only be a matter of hours until we would be feasting, and I would be drinking my grape juice. I had such a cottonmouth these last two days, and I started getting cramps from not having water. I felt like I had sand in my mouth when I woke up that last couple of mornings.

It felt great to get into the Sweat Lodge the next morning. After the sweat, we were out in the arbor dancing, and the last Sundancers pierced.

Also, it's the custom on the fourth day of the Sundance for Heyoka's to come out. They are the clowns, and they tease and tempt you with food and water. I was almost wobbling and I was weak, but I just kept praying. Around noon the Heyoka's came out to do their magic and tease us, dressed in funny Indian clown outfits. Their regalia was all mismatched and funny, half bear and half deer, for example, and they were dancing around and teasing us. The Sundance chief came out in a Panama hat, smoking a cigar, with a bucket full of water and a cup. He was throwing water at the Sundancers feet, and as he passed me he threw a cup of water about four feet in the air in front of me.

At this point I was almost hallucinating, and when I looked out at this water it was sparkling and glowing, almost like neon. It went up in the air, and then fell down, slowly, like syrup, and I could almost inhale that water. I could smell it. It was a serious hallucination that I had at that point. I was getting pretty beat, and the Heyoka's weren't helping me any. It was their job to throw water and tease the dancers. This was all in fun and even funnier because we knew we were close to the end of the Sundance. We would be drinking and feasting soon, so we took it in the sporting way it was meant, and didn't let it get to us.

Finally, I saw the sun go down, and knew it wouldn't be long before this year's Sundance would be over. I saw the Sundance Chief standing in the middle of the arbor yelling "Hoca, Hoca". We all picked up our pipes and ran to the Tree of Life and prayed.

We had a pipe ceremony where all the Sundancers and people from the arbor came out and smoked everyone else's pipe. We shook hands with everyone, and thanked them for being there to support us. It warmed my heart to see the look on some of the peoples' faces when they thanked us for Sundancing for them. I found out that some of these people had fasted for a couple of days while we Sundanced.

When you commit to be a Sundancer, you have to commit yourself to four years. Some of us talked about how we would be back next year and the year after that. I was looking forward to coming back and seeing all the people I had met. During the feast, security brought our coolers that had been put in a big storage area. I drank my grape juice, nice and slow. After that, I drank water, and I felt like my stomach was going to bust. I ate anything and everything.

I called Karen and told her the Sundance was over, and that I had been pierced in the back because the Sundance Chief had advised me it healed sickness in the family.

The ironic thing was, when I spoke to my Mom after I called Karen, she told me that my Dad had checked himself into the Veteran's Hospital the last day of the Sundance, and he didn't even know I was at the Sundance. He had been dry for three days. The longest he had ever been sober in his 67 years was three straight weeks. He had been an alcoholic since he was 16 years of age. I know the Sundance had some bearing on it. The same time I was dancing and praying for his sickness, he checked himself into the hospital. I don't believe in coincidences.

The Creator makes things happen for a reason. He stayed dry for three months, and then he went on a drunk, although I don't think he's drinking as much as he used to. My point being, you can only pray for someone so much, and then the person has to help himself. I still pray for him and he continues to get better. He has slowed down his drinking considerably.

I made it back to my second Sundance in 1995, and this time, I took my brother Dale. At my second Sundance I asked Dennis Banks if he would pierce me, and he said he would be honored. It was rough going for my brother. He made it through the first day, and then he got ill and had to drop out. I felt bad for him so I gifted him my eagle bone whistle which I had two strong Sundances with to help him through his next four years. He was very emotional and thanked me for my support.

It made me feel good to know he was in the arbor watching me dance for him and the rest of our relations. I went to the Sundance Chief during the second Sundance and I told him what I had experienced since 1994. I told him I had a vision where I was told I had to hang. No one had ever hung at Pipestone. They either pulled from the Tree of Life or dragged the skulls. He said that if I was told to hang he wanted to grant my request.

When we got the Tree of Life up during the second Sundance, the Sundance Chief came out and asked who wanted to hang. I told him it was me, and he told me to tie my rope off on this side so we know where to tie the piece that goes across the Sundance tree to support me.

I pierced and I hung on the fourth day, which was a very spiritual experience. Dennis Banks and another Indian brother had danced out to the Tree of Life. Dennis pierced me and got me hooked up to the ropes. Then they had three or four Indian brothers on each side of a log that my rope was tied off to. Once you're hooked up, they back off and leave you up in the air and hold you there until you break free. When I left the ground and was up in the air I had two eagle wing fans, one in each hand. It was really rough going for me, but I no sooner left the ground than I had my vision. There are some Indian brothers who have danced numerous times and never had a vision. I consider myself to be very fortunate to have had a vision, it is one of the greatest experiences I ever had and I will carry it with me throughout my life.

Unfortunately, according to Sundance religion, a Sundancer who has a vision, can only share his vision with another Sundancer (unless the Creator tells you otherwise). I decided to share my vision with my brother Dale.

I feel very honored to have that vision. It totally turned my way of thinking around. I'm looking forward to the next two Sundances. I know I will always be a Sundancer, whether I pierce again after the fourth time or not. After you pierce four times, you are not required to pierce again if you don't feel you want to. Some people do and some don't. Some people just keep going to the Sundances and dance. It's whatever you want to do after that fourth time. I'm just going to leave it in the hands of the Creator.

Between 1994 and 1995 I changed my ways a lot. I'm on that spiritual road...the Red Road...the Sundance Road. I look to the pipe for a lot of my prayers, and I'm living up to my last name more than ever.

It was a whole new year for me, and I'm a different person. I remember other Sundancers telling me that after you've Sundanced, you'll never be the same. The way I was, I couldn't believe I wouldn't be the same; that after only one Sundance my life would totally change. But, that's exactly what did happen. My life took a total turnaround. I'm living in a spiritual way, going to sweat lodges, and keeping up with my spirituality.

Between the spiritual Walk for Justice and my two Sundances, I felt my journey had come full circle. At my second Sundance I had a naming ceremony. My Indian, given name was Good Wolf, and now my name is changed to Harry "Good Wolf" Kindness III. I'm honored to have that name and I will carry it with me as long as I live and continue to try and live up to all that the word means.

As above, so below.

AUTHOR'S NOTE

As of this writing, in the early part of 1999, Leonard Peltier is still incarcerated at Leavenworth Penitentiary and is scheduled for a parole hearing. He is still awaiting Presidential Clemency after eight years, and countless pleas from all over the world for his release. We continue to pray for him and ask you to do the same. Or contact your local politicians to try and help get Leonard out. You can make a difference even with one small voice. Make your voice join countless other voices to stop this injustice.

I am now a full fledged Sundancer and Pipe Carrier which took four years to complete, and is a commitment forever.

Maybe after you've walked this journey with me, you will feel differently toward the Mother Earth and your fellow man. You can change things that are happening in this world, like I did and others since. It's time we all realized that the "me" generation has died, and we truly are all one, living in the same home. Our planet is in serious need of our help to try and restore her health and beauty. If we don't take care of her, we'll all die.

Pray for your red brothers and sisters, for they are the "Keepers of the Earth" and have long been ignored. Pray for others, pray that you become more spiritual and pray for our planet. Give thanks to the Creator for another day and the blessings that were brought to you. If we all changed our thinking just a little bit, and prayed more the entire planet would change and fear of tomorrow would disappear. Then we would have something to leave the generations to come, that would be promising and beautiful, like the Creator intended.

Think about it and maybe someday, somewhere we'll meet again - sometime . . . on another trail.

Mitakuye Oyasin
(All my relations)

Harry "Goodwolf"Kindness - February 11, 1994
on Alcatraz Island, Calif., where
American Indian Movement members celebrated
a sunrise ceremony to start the
"Walk For Justice"

**American Indian Movement members and
supporters gather for a group shot in the high
desert of Nevada.**

**Goodwolf in the Nevada desert during a
snowstorm
braving the elements and nature.**

**Goodwolf setting up his tent after a day's walk for a night's rest off
Highway 50, Nevada - the
loneliest highway in the world!**

**Staff carrier, Dale Van Fleet (Mojave Indian),
myself and walkers on a windy day
outside of Reno, Nevada**

Walkers stop for a moment in Utah

**Dennis Banks, co-founder of A.I.M. addresses
the group before the start of another
morning walk.**

**White Buffalo on the game farm
outside of Gunnison, Colorado**

Goodwolf holding Eagle Staff after coming down from Monarch Pass, 11,312 feet. After encountering blizzard-like conditions.

Group holding a drum ceremony on the site of the Sand Creek massacre in Colorado.

**Early morning mist rises off the ground as
walkers start their day.**

**On the morning we began our last mile into
Washington, D.C. The media was there to cover
the event.**

A.I.M. members, walkers and supporters cross over the Potomac River into Washington D.C. to take part in Peltier Rally

A.I.M. members and supporters at the Walk For Justice Rally for Leonard Peltier, dressed in regalia and displaying banners

A.I.M. members and supporters at the Walk For Justice Rally for Leonard Peltier, dressed in regalia and displaying banners

**Goodwolf and Ernie Stevens Jr., a member of the
Oneida Tribe at the D.C. Rally**

**Goodwolf with Kris Kristofferson who attended
the rally to support the Walk For Justice**

**Goodwolf with the Reverend Jesse Jackson
who attended the Peltier Freedom Weekend
Rally**

L-R: Floyd Crow Westerman, Harry "Goodwolf" Kindness and Dennis Banks (co-founder of American Indian Movement), gather for a moment at the Peltier Freedom Rally.

Last day - July 15, 1994
Good Wolf in full regalia, holding the
"Walk for Justice" Eagle Staff.

252

The word "Wo-Pila" is a Lakota word meaning, "deeply grateful" or a very special thank you, usually directed at the Creator.

If you cannot find this book in your library or bookstore, please contact us at:

Wo-Pila Publishing
P.O. Box 8966
Erie, Pa. 16505-0966

1-800-STONE-22

Thank-you